GOVERNMENT BY CHOICE

Government By Choice

INVENTING THE UNITED STATES CONSTITUTION

═══════════

Elizabeth P. McCaughey

WITH

Preface by Warren E. Burger

Chief Justice of the United States, Retired

AND

Foreword by Senator Daniel Patrick Moynihan

The New-York Historical Society

IN ASSOCIATION WITH

Basic Books, Inc., Publishers   New York

Library of Congress Cataloging-in-Publication Data

McCaughey, Elizabeth P., 1948–
  Government by choice.

  1. United States.   Constitutional Convention (1787).
2. United States—Constitutional history.   I. Title.
KF4520.M45   1987   342.73′029   87–47505
ISBN 0–465–02683–4   347.30229

The New-York Historical Society's exhibition on the Bicentennial of the Constitution has been supported through generous
grants from many individual donors and from:

The National Endowment for the Humanities
William and Flora Hewlett Foundation
J M Foundation

Additional funding for programs related to this exhibition has
been provided through the generosity of:

Country Home Magazine
General Motors Corporation
Newmont Mining Corporation

Preface

THE New-York Historical Society is to be congratulated both for its excellent exhibition on the history of the Constitution and for the publication of its fine commemorative catalogue. Both will contribute to the national effort to make the Constitution Bicentennial a history and civics lesson for all of us.

I am particularly impressed by the historical scholarship reflected in the essay by Dr. Elizabeth McCaughey, the Society's guest curator. Dr. McCaughey has provided a highly readable account of the Philadelphia Convention of 1787, which produced what the British statesman William Ewart Gladstone called "the most wonderful work ever struck off . . . by the brain and purpose of man." Almost everyone recognizes that the founders intended to establish a government structure that would prevent abuses of power, which led them to incorporate the notions of separation of powers and checks and balances—largely borrowed from Montesquieu—as promi-

nent features of the Constitution. Dr. McCaughey persuasively argues that the government structure created by the Constitution was also deliberately designed to give national leaders sufficient independence from parochial and regional special interest groups on the more important matters, so that they could govern in the best interests of the entire country. This thesis is consistent with the opposition of men like James Madison and Thomas Jefferson to federal subsidies for particular segments of society.

In short, Dr. McCaughey's essay, like the Society's exhibition, will provide valuable insights into the origins of the Constitution. If either provokes debate, so much the better.

Warren E. Burger

Foreword

BEFORE this bicentennial year is out I expect we shall all of us hear more than once Gladstone's celebrated assessment of the American constitution as "... the most wonderful work ever struck off at a given time by the brain and purpose of man." But let us take care that the thought not become overfamiliar or even tedious. It is probably true.

The delegates who gathered at Philadelphia undertook to resume the experiment with self-government that began in Greece and continued in Rome for nearly seven hundred years, until Caesar put an end to it in 49 B.C. They knew what the odds were, given what Madison termed "the fugitive and turbulent existence of . . . ancient republics." But they made the bet, took the risk, accepted the challenge—choose your own term—not as gamblers, nor yet adventurers, still less as desperate men with one last chance. Quite the contrary. They recommended the experiment *as scholars*, confident that the new knowledge of the

"science of politics" would enable them to design a system of representative government that—this time—would endure.

And it has endured! There are, at this moment, 159 members of the United Nations. Of these only 7 both existed in 1914 and have not had their form of government changed by internal or external violence since 1914. Of these, the United States of America, still functioning under that Constitution of 1787, is incomparably the largest and most important. Under that Constitution we have grown to be the leader of the democratic nations of the world, of which, not unconnected with our example, there are now many. The count was one when this nation got started. (An imperfect democracy, to be sure, but an implicit one.)

What was this "new science of politics?" Martin Diamond has described it well:

This great new claim rested upon a new and aggressively more "realistic" idea of human nature. Ancient and medieval thought and practice were said to have failed disastrously by clinging to illusions regarding how men ought to be. Instead, the new science would take man as he actually is, would accept as primary in his nature the self-interestedness and passion displayed by all men everywhere and, precisely on that basis, would work out decent political solutions.

And where will it be found? In their writings, of course! Let us be clear on this. The men who wrote our Constitution were learned men who could not conceive of a stable republic governed by other than learned men. Concerned that the level of public discourse be maintained, they asserted that the right to publish books and to read books be guaranteed in the *First* Amendment. The *Second* provides for the right of the people to keep and bear arms so that the militia might be maintained.

It is just that spirit and conviction which led to the establishment of the New-York Historical Society in 1804. Few institutions can boast more nationally significant original manuscripts, documents, portraits, and furniture pertinent to the creation of the Constitution. Here let us insist on the importance of *things* in reconstructing that time. Roam about this exhibition. Read the faces of the founders as well as their letters! See where they sat; sense how it seemed.

As a New York senator I would call especial attention to the exhibits containing works of Rufus King, who with Philip Schulyer, was elected to the newly created Senate on July 16, 1789. King, whose grave is to be found in a lovely churchyard in Jamaica (not far from his then country mansion) had a remarkable and hugely productive public life. The Society has his detailed account of the actual debates of the Philadelphia Convention—apart from Madison's journals, the only comprehensive source of information as to what of late has come to be termed the "original intent" of the founders. In this connection I would call attention to the fact that King's notes make clear beyond any doubt that the Convention determined to establish a "national" government, not a confederation. One essential detail is that senators, although chosen by state legislatures, would vote individually and not as a pair representing their state. But I seem to be getting into a contemporary argument! I'll stop then, but without apology. The arguments are as real today as they were then. The only difference is that in this age the consequences of coming up with the wrong answers are far, far greater.

GOVERNMENT BY CHOICE

Rembrandt Peale. *George Washington*, 1835. Oil on canvas. Bequest of Caroline Phelps Stokes. 1910.3.

On May 25th, the delegates began the great debate by unanimously electing George Washington to be president of the Convention. His presence lent enormous prestige and legitimacy to the Convention's work.

Inventing
the Constitution

May 15–July 26, 1787

G UIDED by candlelight, George Washington stepped into his coach before dawn on May 8, 1787, and began the four-day journey from Mount Vernon to Philadelphia. Without Washington's decision, after lengthy and anxious consideration, to take part in the Constitutional Convention at Philadelphia, there would be only a dismal tale of another failed effort to strengthen the Confederation government. For as James Monroe told Thomas Jefferson that summer, nothing but the presence of the nation's savior in war and unifying symbol could "overawe" the dissensions within the Convention and secure the people's approval of whatever plan the framers recommended.[1] A true story has no beginning or end. Where to pick up or leave off being a matter of choice, the story of the United States Constitution is best commenced with General Washington.

In September 1786, representatives from New York, New Jersey, Delaware, and Pennsylvania, under the leadership of the Virginians, had issued the call for the Philadelphia meeting. All thirteen states were invited to send delegates the following May in order "to render the constitution of the federal government adequate to the exigencies of the union." Washington's closest advisors had warned him, for the nation's sake, not to squander his reputation by attending the illegal and probably unsuccessful meeting.[2] Under the Articles of Confederation, the authority to recommend changes in government belonged to Congress alone. In February 1787, Congress gave its tardy sanction to the meeting. Still Washington was urged to be cautious. At first, Congressman James Madison had implored Washington to come to Philadelphia in May. "Your name," Madison told the retired general, would be "a mark of the earnestness of Virginia, and an invitation to the most select characters from every part of the Confederacy" to attend. Yet in April Madison wondered whether it would be more prudent for Washington to stay away from the Convention until a "judgment" about its character could be made. True friends, the Congressman wrote, did not wish the General to be involved in any "abortive undertaking." By then, Washington had resolved to go to Philadelphia as the head of the Virginia delegation. One American statesman wrote to Lafayette that Washington had committed his fame "to the mercy of events. Nothing but the critical situation of his country would have induced him to so hazardous a conduct."[3]

Washington lamented that the nation's future had never seemed more clouded. Government was fast giving way to "anarchy and confusion." For seven years he had insisted that trying to uphold the dignity of the new nation in European councils and promote prosperity and union at home without an adequately constituted government was "attempting the impossible." The Articles of Confederation, which were drafted by Congress in 1777 and ratified by the states from 1777 to 1781, established only a Congress with meager lawmaking authority and relied on the state governors and state courts to carry out the nation's laws and treaties. Congress had no authority to raise troops and provisions for war, to tax, or to regulate foreign commerce, and the nation lacked a permanent executive and judiciary.

After the Revolution, the war-weary states turned inward, refusing to grant Congress the authority, the funds, and the self-respect to meet its peacetime obligations. The Confederation government met in New York at the old City Hall, close to the "burnt district" where nearly every

building had been defaced or destroyed by the British occupation. There was only languor and despair in Congress. Time and again the infrequent and unpredictable attendance of the state delegations embarrassed the government and suspended its proceedings. Annually the Congress determined how much money each state ought to contribute to the nation's expenses, but the states paid their requisitions tardily or not at all. In 1786, the funds collected from the states did not pay one-third of the interest on the national debt. Requisitions, Washington noted bitterly, were "little better than a jest." The Congress's helplessness to enforce its agreements with foreign powers humiliated the nation abroad. Despite the terms of the Treaty of Paris ending the Revolutionary War, the state legislators persisted in punishing former loyalists, and state courts failed to compel Americans to repay their prewar debts owed to British creditors. In retaliation, the British refused to evacuate seven military posts in the Northwest Territory. Washington exclaimed in frustration, "If you tell the legislatures they have violated the treaty of peace and invaded the prerogatives of the Confederacy, they will laugh in your face."[4]

Even more distressing was the reluctance of the states to invest the Confederation with adequate powers over the nation's commerce. Without this authority, Congress could neither tax trade to pay its enormous domestic and foreign debts nor defend American shipping against the discriminatory restrictions imposed by other nations. British Orders in Council that excluded American vessels from the British West Indies dealt a heavy blow to America's economy. The New England carrying trade languished, Southern agricultural exporters stood at the mercy of British

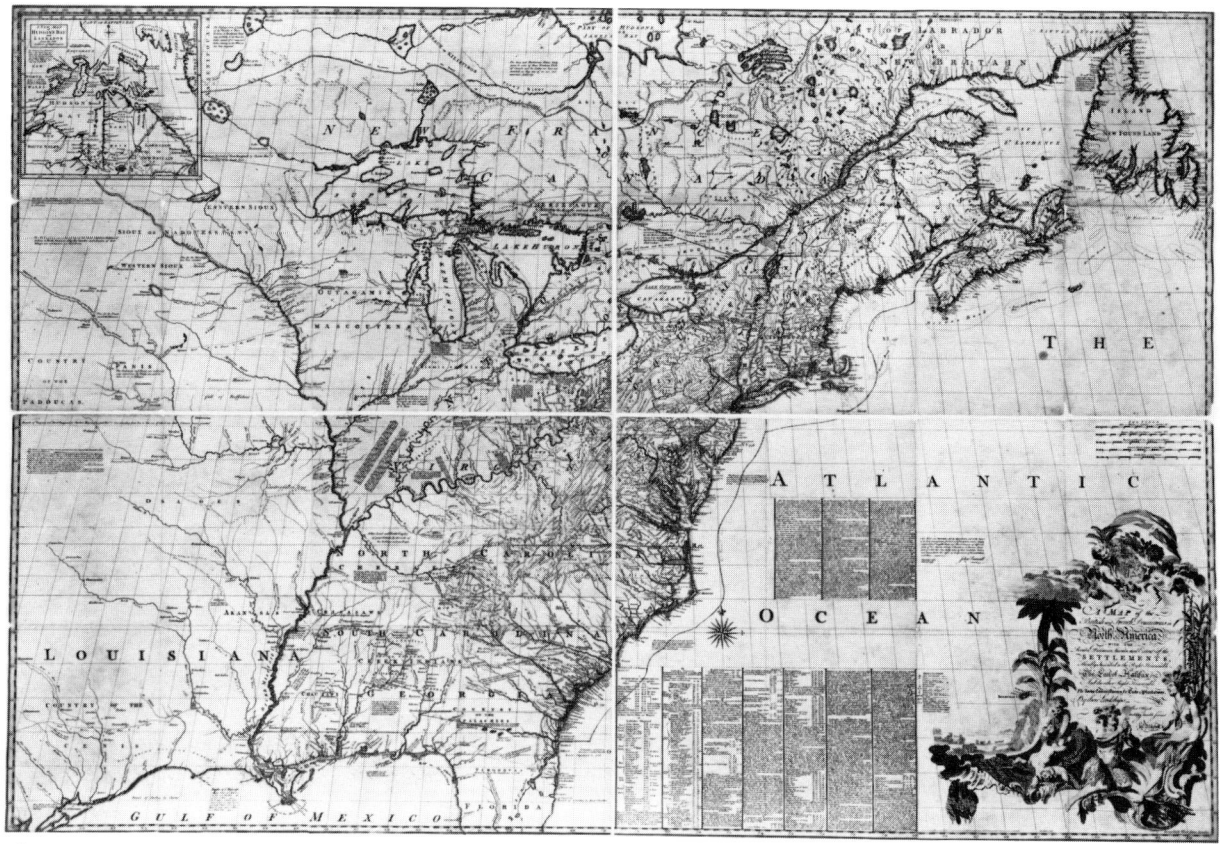

John Jay's copy of "A map of the British and French Dominions in North America . . . ," drawn by John Mitchell in 1755. (Third edition, London, 1755). Gift of Peter Jay.

In November 1782, John Jay carried this map to Paris to negotiate a treaty with Great Britain ending the War of Independence. On the map Jay marked by hand the boundaries of the new United States.

The American government established by the Articles of Confederation was powerless to compel the states to honor the terms of the treaty. The states failed to protect loyalists from harsh reprisals and to compel the repayment of debts owed to British creditors. In turn, the British refused to honor United States boundaries and evacuate Niagara, Detroit, and other garrisons on United States soil. In 1786, George Washington told Jay, "Your sentiments, that our affairs are drawing rapidly to a crisis, accord with my own. . . . If you tell the [state] Legislatures they have violated the treaty of peace and invaded the prerogatives of the Confederacy, they will laugh in your face."

shippers, and the republic's balance of trade worsened. Congress applied to the states for the necessary authority to retaliate against the British Orders in Council. Sectional jealousies and distrust of the central government defeated the request. Instead the individual states tried to impose their own retaliatory restrictions on British trade, attempts that produced chaos and ill will among the states but no concessions from abroad. Historians have seen, in retrospect, that the Confederation government accomplished a great deal, including winning a war and securing peace on advantageous terms, but the men of the times saw only a mounting crisis. Even antinationalists such as Maryland's Luther Martin, who would storm out of the Convention and later oppose the new Constitution, readily admitted that the Confederation was "weak, contemptibly weak." Washington deplored the "local prejudices and policies" that frustrated the national good. On March 31, just days after he had notified Virginia's Governor Edmund Randolph that he would attend the Constitutional Convention, Washington wrote privately to the young Congressman engaged in planning the meeting, James Madison. He urged Madison to "probe the defects of the Constitution to the bottom" and provide "radical cures." The time had passed for mere "temporizing expedients."[5]

After three days of travel, Washington reached the Susquehanna, but the river was so swollen with spring rain that a day of waiting was necessary before crossing. On the evening of May 13, his coach neared the edge of the city. There, smartly assembled, were the City Light Horse Infantry, fitted in white breeches and shiny black hats. Tolling church bells and excited onlookers greeted the General as his coach made its way to Fifth and Market streets. Washington hurried to the home of Mrs. Mary House, who presided over a little empire of attached brick and clapboard houses that provided rooms and apartments for paying guests. Waiting there anxiously was Madison, whose arrival in Philadelphia ten days earlier had occasioned no public fanfare.[6]

In Congress Madison had earned a reputation for hard work and competence. Outside of Congress, few men knew of him. At the outset, other delegates at the Convention would mistakenly call him Mr. Matthewson or Mr. Maddson.[7] He had been born into circumstances comfortable, but not remarkably wealthy, by Southern standards. The chronic failure of the state to pay his salary as a congressman had compelled him to borrow money more than once from Haym Salomon, a wealthy Phil-

adelphia merchant who loaned funds at no interest to needy members of Congress. Compared with the austere dignity and commanding stature of Washington, Madison was a small, shy, almost common figure. He wore ruffles at his neck and wrists and powder on his neatly arranged hair, but the elegance was undercut by his ruddy complexion and squat—a mere five feet six inches—muscular build.[8] His appearance gave no clue that this man had already set his mind to ruling the Convention and shaping the new republic.

For many months, Madison had prepared for the event, probing the histories of ancient and modern polities and setting down his diagnosis of the republic's ills in a memorandum, "Vices of the Political System of the U. States." In April and May, he had sent his outline of a new national government to General Washington, Governor Randolph, and Thomas Jefferson, who bridled at being far off in Paris as America's minister to France when more important things were about to happen at home. Madison discarded the principle of confederation entirely and sketched a government of three branches— a legislature, executive, and judiciary—that would act on the citizens of the United States without relying on the voluntary cooperation of state governments. As the Confederation crisis grew, a government of three branches had been talked about by others, among them George Washington, John Jay of New York, and Rufus King of Massachusetts.

What made Madison's plan new was his clear vision of a "national" government, that is, a government established by the authority of the people, rather than the states, elected by the people, and ruling the people directly. Equally distinctive was Madison's zeal to see the plan accomplished without regard to the "local or tem-

Asher B. Durand. *James Madison*, 1835. Oil on canvas. Gift of the New York Gallery of Fine Arts. 1858.10.

James Madison campaigned tirelessly for a Constitutional Convention. "What may be the result of this political experiment cannot be foreseen," he confessed to Jefferson. But the "mortal diseases" of the existing Confederation and "the unwise and wicked" state laws imperiling property and personal liberties necessitated a change of government. For many months, Madison read the histories of ancient and modern republics and labored over a complete plan of national government. By presenting his Virginia Plan on the opening day, Madison seized the opportunity to guide the Convention away from a mere revision of the Articles of Confederation. He was determined to lead the Union out of a weak confederation into a national system of government.

porary prejudices'' that had frustrated earlier attempts. The new government was also to wield vastly increased lawmaking authority, preserving the power of the states only where they could be ''subordinately useful.'' Madison reasoned that because only the state legislatures had been called upon to ratify the Articles of Confederation, the authority of the Articles was never superior to any other act of a state legislature. The new constitution, reasoned Madison, had to be ratified by special popular conventions and derive its ''validity'' from the will of the sovereign people. Additionally, Madison deplored the injustice of the voting rule in the old Congress, where Virginia, though thirteen times as populous as Delaware, had the same influence. The equal representation of every state, regardless of its size, had to yield to a system of proportionality that allotted voting power to each state according to its population. Zealous to achieve what was right, Madison blindly predicted that this change could be accomplished ''without much difficulty.''[9]

In ''Vices,'' his memorandum on the existing system, Madison devoted more discussion to the ''vicious legislation'' enacted in the states than to the weaknesses of the Confederation government. In many states, factions—majorities united by some passion or interest—seized control of the legislature and turned it to their own advantage, neglecting the public good and injuring the personal and property rights of individuals. One religious sect oppressed another. Farmers clamored for laws injurious to merchants. Debtors intruded on the rights of creditors. Demands were heard for laws to postpone the obligations owed to lenders and for paper money, though it would inflate the economy with a nearly worthless currency. Whatever new plan of government the Convention devised, Madison wrote, had to provide an antidote to the rampant injustices committed by self-serving factions.[10]

All spring, Madison considered remedies for the pernicious power of self-interested majorities. The new national legislature, he suggested to Jefferson in March, ought to be armed with a complete veto over state legislation ''in all cases whatsoever.''[11]

Madison reasoned that the national legislature would seldom fall under the control of a self-seeking faction. In a nation so vast and embracing so many different religious sects, regional cultures, and commercial interests, it was unlikely that a majority of the representatives would ever unite on any principle except the common good.[12] Madison was alarmed to see an idea gaining ground in the newspapers and in the private conversations of American statesmen that the Union ought to be dismembered into three or four homogeneous republics. The idea, Washington was told by one of his aides, would be offered at the Convention. Madison deemed it a great evil. With increasing frequency the question was asked whether any government, except a despotism, could govern a nation of Southern planters, Appalachian farmers, and New England merchants.[13] In ''Vices,'' Madison insisted that the diversity of the nation ought to be regarded as an advantage, because it promised to impede the politics of self-interest. In a great national legislature, a multitude of clashing factions would cancel one another and produce a stalemate.[14]

Madison wanted to impede the politics of self-interest, but he also wanted an energetic, national government, not a government of inaction. In the last paragraph of ''Vices,'' he went beyond remedies for faction to suggest in a barely formulated way

Rembrandt Peale. *Thomas Jefferson*, 1805. Oil on canvas. Gift of Thomas J. Bryan. 1867.306.

From his diplomatic post in Paris, Jefferson read with interest the latest reports about the movement for constitutional reform. But he felt none of the urgency that impelled his friends Washington and Madison to act. Jefferson was unshaken by Shays' Rebellion and reflected calmly that "a little rebellion now and then is a good thing." He reminded Washington that the monarchies of Europe made government in America, "with all its defects," seem "the happiest political situation" on earth.

his prescription for good national government. He did not mention the separation of powers or checks and balances. The answer was leadership. The offices of the national government had to be filled with men noble enough to put the public good ahead of private gain and competent enough to govern wisely. The task of the constitution makers would be to design a government that attracted the most talented, public-minded men to public office and to provide a system of elections that consistently rewarded them.[15]

The terror of Shays' Rebellion awakened complacent men to conclude, as Madison had reasoned much earlier, that the property and personal rights of individuals must be shielded from desperate majorities. From September 1786 to the next February, debt-ridden farmers in Massachusetts, angered by the scarcity of hard currency to pay their taxes and mortgages and fearing foreclosures and debtors' prison, had resorted to mob action. They had forced the courts to close and even had taken up arms to attack the federal arsenal at Springfield. Almost everyone, of whatever political temperament, deplored the lawlessness and violence. Madison called it "distressing beyond measure." His political rival in Virginia, Richard Henry Lee, who would oppose the new Constitution, abhorred the Shaysites as "little insurgents, men in debt who want no law and who want a share of the property of others." Jefferson stood alone in his blithe judgment that "a little rebellion now and then" was a good thing. Rulers, he said, had to be "warned from time to time that their people preserve the spirit of resistance."[16] Though leading nationalists throughout the states had earlier agreed that a radical revision of the Articles of Confederation was desperately needed,

Shays' Rebellion turned the eyes of the previously undecided toward Philadelphia.

On May 14, the morning after General Washington's arrival and the day appointed for the Convention to begin, five of the Virginia delegates walked over to the Pennsylvania State House and entered the East Room. There Washington had been appointed Commander-in-Chief twenty-two years earlier, as the Continental Congress armed the colonies, not yet a nation, for war. There, in his absence, the Continental Congress had debated and finally confronted the perils of independence. Sun streamed through the tall windows and bathed the huge chamber in warm light. The room was quiet, the rows of writing tables unused. Only the Pennsylvania delegation was in attendance. As seven states were necessary for a quorum, the Pennsylvanians and Virginians agreed to reassemble every afternoon to count new arrivals. It had rained for nearly a week, Madison reminded himself, and surely it was the bad roads, not indifference, that kept men away.[17]

Mornings, the Virginians were huddled over Madison's plan, determined to reconcile their differences and present a united front when the meeting began. With General Washington and Madison were George Wythe, the esteemed professor of law at the College of William and Mary; George Mason, draftsman of the Virginia Declaration of Rights; Governor Edmund Randolph; Judge John Blair, a mild nationalist; and Dr. James McClurg, a physician and valued friend of Madison. Randolph, for one, proposed that a few changes be "grafted on the old Confederation" form of government. Madison and Washington argued unrelentingly for an entirely new scheme. Never mind what the public might expect, the pair implored. Create the best possible system and have faith that in time its merits would be recognized. Randolph admitted that these intense morning sessions changed his thinking. On one issue Madison was forced to compromise, against his liking. The Virginia Plan would empower the national legislature to nullify a state law on constitutional grounds only, though Madison firmly believed that the power should operate "in all cases whatsoever."[18]

Days passed, the delegations failed to appear. Madison wrote somberly to his father that he was "suffering" with disappointment. Their tardiness, lamented Washington, soured the tempers of the men already there. Rufus King was in a hurry to establish "a more permanent and vigorous government." He fumed that it was mortifying to be the only New England delegate in attendance. At last, on Friday, May 25, seven states were fully represented, enough for a quorum. Business began. The prestige of the still meager gathering soared when Washington agreed to preside as president of the Convention.[19]

A secretary was also chosen, Major William Jackson of Philadelphia. Madison suspected that Jackson would keep a mere skeletal record of the proposals and votes. Perceiving that this was a meeting with destiny, Madison knew that more would be needed. The inspired Virginian took a seat at the front of the room and began to write. At every session that summer, Madison would be seen bowed over the writing table, recording in phrases and abbreviations the substance of the day's debates.[20] Five other delegates kept notes of the proceedings they attended. Rufus King's were the best of these, though less complete than Madison's. These other notes have enabled historians to identify the unfortunate changes Madison made to his records later

in life and to confirm his amazingly unbiased story. The account you are about to read is based on the notes taken by the framers, especially James Madison.[21]

Signs of Promise

When the Convention assembled again on Monday, May 28, nine more delegates took their seats. Crowds outside the State House and the delegates within looked on as Dr. Benjamin Franklin, who had been too feeble to attend on Friday, was carried into the State House in a sedan chair. The eighty-one-year-old statesman, the oldest man at the Convention, peered back through the glass windows of the little carriage which he had brought back from Paris. It was set on two long poles and derived its motion from the lumbering strides of four prisoners out of the nearby jail who balanced the poles on their shoulders.[22]

The day's task was to agree to the formal rules of proceeding. No delegate would speak twice on a question until everyone else who desired to be heard had spoken. All committees would be elected by ballot. All questions would be decided by a vote of the states represented, each delegation casting one vote. Before the Convention began, Gouverneur Morris of Pennsylvania had pressed the Virginians to insist on giving the most populous states more votes at the Convention. But the Virginians had held back, realizing that if the small states were angered at the outset, the opportunity to present the Virginia Plan as the basis of the Convention's discussions might be lost, or worse still, the Convention might break up.[23]

The most important rule was adopted

the following morning: nothing spoken or decided within the Convention could be disclosed to anyone. The delegates wanted the freedom to consider the boldest proposals and to change their minds and votes freely without worrying what their political rivals might say or what half-formed idea might alarm the public. Sentries were posted at the doorways, and despite the summer heat, the windows were nailed shut. Jefferson, aching to know what his notable friends were deciding in his absence, was "sorry they began their deliberation by so abominable a precedent." "Nothing can justify this example but the innocence of their intentions, & ignorance of the value of public discussions." Newspaper men responded more sympathetically. The secrecy rule was "a happy omen," said one editor, that the "spirit of party" would not taint the deliberations. Americans expressed no discontent with "the concealment," Madison told Jefferson.[24] That summer the rule would be broken no more than four times, and only in private letters, never to the press.

On May 29, Edmund Randolph rose to present the Virginia Plan. He was an instantly likable figure, almost six feet tall, with loose, flowing, dark hair and a youthful, handsome face. As his eyes surveyed the room, he saw many promising signs. John Dickinson of Delaware and Elbridge Gerry of Massachusetts had arrived that morning, bringing the total number of delegates to forty, and another fifteen were expected. Rhode Island, long notorious for defying Congress, refused to send a delegation, but the twelve other states had answered the call, a sufficient number to endow the Convention with legitimacy.[25]

The Convention, Randolph could plainly see, had attracted energetic nationalists. Men such as Patrick Henry of Virginia and Samuel Adams of Massachusetts, who doubted the wisdom or possibility of erecting a strong, central government, had refused to attend. Randolph's gaze fell momentarily on the New York table, where Alexander Hamilton sat uncomfortably beside his arch political rival, the antinationalist Robert Yates. Hamilton wished that John Jay and James Duane, proven nationalists, had been named to the delegation. Instead, John Lansing, a close political ally of New York's Governor George Clinton, would soon be arriving to support Yates. The New York delegation would be troublesome, until July 10, when Lansing and Yates would storm out in protest and never return. Maryland had also appointed two antinationalists, Luther Martin and John Francis Mercer, who were hand-in-glove with the powerful leader of the state's paper money faction, but they were outnumbered by three other delegates with national dispositions. "In general," the Virginians observed, most of the delegates viewed the nation's situation as "peculiarly critical" and were prepared for "a total change of the federal system."[26]

Randolph was heartened to see the room filled with so many men of great and well-deserved reputations. The anxious Madison appraised the gathering as "the best contribution of talents the States could make for the occasion."[27] Randolph believed that the future strength and dignity of the nation was at stake. The delegates were impressed with the seriousness of their task. Thirty-nine had served in Congress, daily witnessing the embarrassment and inadequacies of the Confederation government. Many of the delegates apprehended that even more was at stake. Should the Convention fail, Franklin feared, "it will show that we do not have wisdom enough ... to govern ourselves, and strengthen the opinion of some political writers, that popular governments cannot long support themselves." The precipitous decline of confidence in our rulers and the insecurity of property, Washington worried, might cause the people to lose faith in self-government and succumb to the charms of monarchy or oligarchy. George Mason confessed that before the other delegations arrived, he too had feared that the "evils" arising from popular government in the states would drive the Convention "into the opposite extreme." Mason was relieved to see that the men seated in the State House held firm to republican values.[28] They were committed to inventing a system of self-government that would prove, through example, that government by the people was consistent with what Madison called "the security of private rights and the steady dispensation of Justice."[29]

They would begin with the first principles of government. Those principles, reflected Hamilton, ought to be as discoverable through reason and deliberation as the maxims of geometry or natural science. They would quickly eschew the British model of government as inapplicable to the manners and expectations of Americans. And the names and theories of European philosophers would seldom be mentioned. In 1687, Sir Isaac Newton had discovered the law of gravity. With the same spirit, the delegates assembled one hundred years later in the State House to discover the laws of good government and establish a system of government according to them. In October, when their task was completed, Hamilton would announce its significance to the nation on the opening page of *The Federalist*: "It seems to have been reserved to the people of this country, by their conduct and example, to decide the important ques-

tion, whether societies of men are really capable or not of establishing good government from reflection and choice, or whether they are forever destined to depend for their political constitutions on accident and force."[30]

Modern political scientists look to such informal institutions as political parties and to economic and psychological factors to understand political life. It has been unfashionable in our century to consider the formal institutions of government and their underlying constitution. But the founders believed that the decisions they were to make that summer, as they established the formal offices of government and determined their tenure, powers, and method of selection, would promote public-minded leadership, preserve accountability to the electorate, and deter factionalism. They believed that the design of government made a difference. It was John Adams who expressed their conviction, when he declared that winter, in praise of the delegates' work, that good government depended not on fate, climate, or the preponderance of virtue but instead on a "well ordered constitution."[31]

Randolph spoke with a clearer, steadier voice than his inventive, but shy, colleague James Madison. As Randolph stood before the Convention on the morning of the twenty-ninth, he expressed his regret that it should fall on him, rather than on someone of "longer standing in life and political experience" to begin discussion "on the great subject of their mission." Because Virginia had initiated the call for a convention, the Virginia delegation felt responsible to offer a plan, and Randolph's colleagues had imposed the task on him.[32] Although Governor of Virginia, Randolph was a mere thirty-three years old. Seated before him were men whose involvement in the American cause had begun decades earlier—John Rutledge, William Samuel Johnson, and John Dickinson, who had served together at the Stamp Act Congress in 1765; Elbridge Gerry, Roger Sherman, Robert Morris, James Wilson, George Clymer, Benjamin Franklin, George Read, and George Wythe, who had signed the Declaration of Independence; and other delegates, including the great Washington, who had missed the celebrated signing because they had hurried off to war. Yet it was a youthful boldness that led the Convention at the outset. Despite the distinguished reputations of the framers, most were young, their average age only forty-three. The Virginian who would steer the deliberations with his radical proposals, James Madison, had just turned thirty-six. Young Madison and men of his persuasion, who had come of age during the Continental war effort, were determined to lead the country from a loose confederation into a strong national government. Several of the elder statesmen, such as Franklin, Johnson, Sherman, and Dickinson, whose political careers long antedated the struggle for American unity, would play another role. They were mindful of the local loyalties and fears that impeded union, and they were determined to model a practical government acceptable to all thirteen states. They saw the necessity to listen as well as to lead.[33]

The delegates weighed each word as Randolph read the fifteen resolutions that constituted the Virginia Plan. He began, "Resolved that the articles of Confederation ought to be so corrected & enlarged as to accomplish . . . 'common defence, security of liberty and general welfare.' " The remaining fourteen resolutions called for a two-house legislature with representation in each house proportional to the popula-

tions of the member states, a national executive charged with executing the laws, and a national judiciary. The national legislature was given broad lawmaking powers and the authority to nullify any state law that conflicted with the new national constitution. The Plan provided for the direct election of the lower house by the people but removed the other institutions of government from popular influence. The upper house, executive, and judiciary would be chosen by the lower house. Although under the Articles of Confederation all amendments were to be approved by the state legislatures, the Virginians circumvented the state governments and called upon the people of each state to elect a special convention for the sole purpose of ratifying the new plan.[34] Far from merely revising the Articles of Confederation, the Virginians had completely abandoned the principle of confederation. The new government would be a direct compact with the people because the states had failed to meet their obligations to the nation or even maintain justice and order within their own boundaries. To Gouverneur Morris of Pennsylvania, a firm supporter of Madison's scheme, "State attachments and State importance had been the bane of this Country. We cannot annihilate [these vicious states]; but we may perhaps take out the teeth of the serpents."[35]

The true intent of the Virginia Plan became clear at ten o'clock the next morning. As soon as the delegates had reassembled, Randolph exhorted the Convention to formally resolve, in place of the first resolution offered the previous day, that "a Union of the States merely federal" was inadequate and "that a national Government ought to be established" consisting of a legislature, executive, and judiciary. Randolph's bold request left the delegates stunned and silent. After some time, Gouverneur Morris rose to explain the difference between "federal" and "national." The terms are used synonymously today, but they meant radically different things to the men of 1787. The new national plan did not rest on the "good faith" of the states, Morris said. The government would act directly on the individual citizens. Two of the delegates worried aloud whether the commissions from their states, which charged them to "render the constitution of the federal government adequate to the exigencies of the Union" permitted them to discard the federal system entirely. The old Congress had tardily given its endorsement to the Convention, "for the sole and express purpose of revising the Articles of Confederation."

Roger Sherman of Connecticut spoke next. He was a lean, older man with a plain, country suit, an awkward stance, and a craggy, sharp-featured face. He had risen from humble origins to be a respected

Thirteen-star United States flag. Hand-woven cotton. 1939.559.

American patriots waited almost a year after the Declaration of Independence before giving the new nation a flag. In June 1777, Congress received a petition from the Indian Nation for one sample of the flag of the United States. Three strings of wampum accompanied the request. The congressmen, surprised and embarrassed that the nation had no flag, immediately resolved that the United States be symbolized by thirteen stripes, alternately red and white, and thirteen white stars on a blue ground. Congress did not specify how the stars were to be arranged. The flag pictured here, with twelve stars in a circle and one in the center, was typical of the period 1777–95. It was found in a house in Putnam County, New York.

lawyer and politician in his state, but the words he chose revealed that he was a self-taught man. He admitted that the Articles of Confederation had not given Congress sufficient powers. He was, however, against making "too great inroads on the existing system." It would be wrong to jeopardize the chance for reform by offering resolutions that the states would not approve. Despite these warnings, the majority pressed ahead, agreeing in substance to erect a "national" government with its own legislature, executive, and judiciary.[36]

Randolph proceeded to the next resolution of the Virginia Plan, which allocated representation in the national legislature to each state according to the size of its population. Immediately, George Read of Delaware, the smallest state to attend the Convention, urged that the resolution be postponed. Read was a small-state man with big ideas for the nation. He ardently supported the call for a strong, central government. He was against "patching up the old federal system." Merely enlarging its powers was like "putting new cloth on an old garment." It could not last. At times he was heard to say indiscreetly that the Convention ought to do away with the troublesome state governments altogether. But Delaware had expressly restrained its delegation from agreeing to any change in the voting rule in Congress. If the Convention persisted in the discussion, explained Read, the Delaware men would be compelled to walk out. The majority heeded Read's warning, fearful that the departure of even one state would discredit the Convention in the public's eyes and worse bring the meeting to an end. No one doubted that a bitter struggle for power was ahead. James Madison and Gouverneur Morris gave notice that proportional representation "could not be dispensed with." The rule of equal voting had to "cease" when a national government was "put into place."[37]

The delegates' readiness to undertake a radical change of government was confirmed on May 31, when the Virginians secured a huge majority for Resolution 6, which empowered the national legislature to govern "in all cases" in which the individual states were incompetent. The legendary South Carolina statesman John Rutledge and his youthful colleague Charles Pinckney took the floor in defense of Southern interests. They objected to the vagueness of the term "incompetent" and wanted an exact description of the national legislature's powers. Rutledge and Pinckney privately worried that a government with such broadly defined powers might intrude into the South's most sensitive business, slavery. But so fired was the Convention to pursue the Virginia Plan that even Pinckney's and Rutledge's fellow delegates from the deep South did not recognize the danger. Minutes later, the Convention gave its unanimous approval to a resolution that empowered the national legislators to review and nullify any state law they deemed unconstitutional. One of the pillars of the Virginia Plan was set firmly in place.[38]

They "never once thought of a king"

On June 1, the Convention considered the national executive for the first time. Immediately, James Wilson's firm Scottish voice and towering stature captured the attention of the delegates, as he seized the occasion to present his model of a strong executive branch. Everyone listened intently. Since his arrival in Philadelphia from his native Scotland in 1765, Wilson had earned acclaim as a near-genius of political and legal theory. Every man in the room had read or heard of his 1774 essay challenging the right of the British Parliament to make laws for the American colonies. It was Wilson's model of the executive branch and his own persistence that produced the American presidency, although the title President would not be decided upon until August. Wilson wanted the executive to be an equal and independent branch, not a mere instrument of the national legislature, and to claim a common commission from the legitimate source of all authority, the people themselves. The bold thinker from Pennsylvania had to win the support of the Convention's other leading nationalists, including James Madison, and he was unrelenting until he had succeeded.[39]

It is remarkable that James Madison had given so little thought to the design of the national executive before the Convention met. Madison had long been convinced that the greatest danger of tyranny in a republican government arose from the imbalance of power that was customarily found in republics. The authors of the first state constitution, he believed, had erred in locating all the power in the legislature and putting the executive and judicial offices of government entirely at the mercy of the legislature for their appointment powers. In April 1787, when Madison sent his preliminary sketch of a national government to Randolph and Washington, he had confessed that "a National Executive must also be provided. I have scarcely ventured as yet to form my own opinion either of the manner in which it ought to be constituted or of the authorities with which it ought to be cloathed."

The Plan failed to specify whether a single person or a committee would occupy the office. The executive was to be chosen by the national legislature, and its powers were limited to executing the laws made by the legislature and exercising the "executive rights vested in Congress by the Confederation." So weak was executive authority that Madison provided for a council of revision, joining the Supreme Court justices and the executive together to exert a veto power that, he apprehended, the executive alone could never wield against the legislature.[40]

The timidity of the Virginia Plan was revealed the moment that the Convention began debating how the executive ought to be chosen. Roger Sherman defended the Plan's provision for an appointment by the legislature, arguing that the executive ought to be "absolutely dependent" on the first branch. He "considered the Executive magistracy as nothing more than an institution for carrying the will of the Legislature into effect. The Executive ought to be appointed by and accountable to the Legislature only, which was the depositary of the Supreme will of the Society."[41]

The Scotsman from Pennsylvania rose again, this time to remind the Convention that each institution of government ought to stand independent of the others and possess the confidence of the people. Wilson's voice wavered as he ventured to make a daring announcement that, at least in theory, he favored allowing the people rather than the legislature to choose the executive. He confessed that popular election might appear extraordinary or even "chimerical." Most of the delegates doubted that the people would be sufficiently well informed of statesmen outside their own state to choose the nation's leader. George Mason considered it as "unnatural" to rely on the people to elect the chief magistrate as it would be to "refer a trial of colours to a blind man." How could a farmer from Massachusetts know about the character and qualifications of a statesman from Virginia or Pennsylvania? It was feared that the people would be misled by men more skilled in the art of winning popularity than in the science and ethics of good government.[42]

Wilson stood almost alone in his advocacy of a popular election, but he would not accept defeat. When the meeting adjourned for the day, he walked one block to his home on Chestnut Street. Even the chatter of his six young children added no gaiety to his homecoming. The recent death of his beloved wife, Rachel, filled the house with a bleakness and sorrow that greeted him at the door. That night, Wilson sat alone at his desk and labored over a plan for the indirect election of the national executive. Divide the states into large districts, he reasoned, and allow the people of each district to choose presidential electors, who would ballot for a national executive. The next morning at the State House, his proposal won few adherents, though it would appear in the finished Constitution three months later. The Convention voted eight to two that the national legislature choose the executive for a term of seven years.[43]

The delegates were not ready to consider a popularly elected executive, but neither were they content with Sherman's concept of the chief magistrate as a mere servant of the legislature. Representative government, they hoped, did not have to mean the dominance of an all-powerful legislature. Whether it was possible in a republic to establish a vigorous, independent executive whose authority would reach to the remotest corners of a great nation was the question that challenged the Convention.

When Wilson offered a motion that the "Executive consist of a single person," a sudden quiet filled the room. The delegates continued to exchange uncomfortable glances, and the silence stretched on. A single executive, they feared, would bear an alarming resemblance to a king. The esteemed John Rutledge of South Carolina, who had served at the Stamp Act Congress and the Continental Congress, rose to chide the delegates for their shyness. Whatever opinions they expressed, he reminded them, could be changed later. He declared himself in favor of the motion. "A single man would feel the greatest responsibility and administer the public affairs best." Edmund Randolph sternly declared his opposition. A single magistrate was "the foetus of monarchy." He agreed with many of the delegates that the British form of government was "an excellent fabrick," but the Convention was barred from considering it. The temper and convictions of the American people prohibited any semblance of kingship. He and George Mason advocated an executive consisting of three persons, one chosen from the North, one from the South, and one from the middle states to "quiet the Minds of the People . . . that there will be proper attention paid to their respective concerns." The proposal hinted ominously of the sectional conflict ahead.[44]

Wilson answered Randolph's objections point by point. A single executive, he argued, instead of inviting monarchy, would be the best safeguard against tyranny. One man could be held more accountable for his deeds and misdeeds than a committee. A single executive would be not only the most capable of secrecy and quick action but also the most responsible. To control the legislature, he reasoned, divide it. To control the executive, unite it.[45]

Wilson fended off proposals that the executive be encumbered by a mandatory council of advisors, insisting that a plurality of men would "serve to cover rather than prevent malpractices." The Pennsylvania scholar would often remind his law students at the College of Philadelphia that "the British throne is surrounded by counsellors. . . . Who possesses the executive power? The King. When its baleful emanations fly over the land, who are responsible for this mischief? His ministers." In the United States, the executive would not be "shielded behind the mysterious obscurity" of an official council.[46] Wilson repeated that he did not have kingly prerogatives in mind. Do not confuse the proposal for a single executive with the British monarchy, he said.[47]

Eleven years after the American colonists rebelled against George III and Thomas Paine declared that nature had proved the folly of kingship by giving the British nation "an ass for a lion," the framers were looking for ways to incorporate the advantages of kingship into their plan of government without actually returning to monarchy. It was uncertain, admitted the distinguished Delaware statesman John Dickinson, whether the blessings of constitutional monarchy could ever be duplicated in a republic. Perhaps a firm executive could only be a king. Every delegate in the room had read and still remembered Dickinson's famous revolutionary tracts against British oppression. Now they listened to him speculate on the possibility of a lasting republican government. To despair would be fruitless, Dickinson exhorted. "If ancient republics have been found to flourish for a moment only & then vanish forever, it only proves that they were badly constituted; and that we ought to seek for every remedy for their dis-

eases."[48] A majority of the delegates felt a daring confidence in their ability to achieve with reason and the scientific principles of government what history seemed to say was not possible. On June 4, they voted seven states to four for a single executive, a bold decision from which they would never retreat. When, in August, the public's impatience with the ongoing labors of the Convention gave rise to a rumor that the delegates had sent to Europe and awaited a royal leader, the Convention would deliver a message to the newspapers, that they could not say what they were doing, but they could announce that they "never once thought of a king."[49]

The quiet presence of George Washington added greatly to the delegates' confidence. The Georgia delegate Pierce Butler later remembered that many of the framers "cast their eyes towards General Washington" as they crafted the executive branch and "shaped their ideas of the powers to be given to a President by their opinions" of him. Again and again the framers affirmed that they had to take a "permanent view of the subject" and erect a government for future generations. Everyone at the Convention and outside knew who the nation's first leader would be, regardless of the design of the office. "The first man, put at the helm will be a good one," Franklin declared on June 4. "Nobody knows what sort may come afterwards."[50] The availability of Washington, a revered leader, would be critical to the plan's acceptance. Gouverneur Morris would remind Washington in October that if the idea gained ground that he would not accept the highest office "it would prove fatal" to the federal plan. The nation, Morris wrote, was prepared to elevate Washington to a position in which "they would not readily put any other person."[51]

Alexandre Roslin. *Benjamin Franklin*, ca. 1789–90 (after Joseph S. Duplessis). Oil on canvas. The Louis Dorr Fund. 1892.8.

Benjamin Franklin, renowned in Europe and America for his achievements in science, art, literature, and public service, and at eighty-one the oldest delegate, declared the Convention to be "the most august and respectable Assembly he was ever in in his life."

In June, as the delegates drafted and argued about the nation's executive, they understood with increasing clarity how to make a strong head of state without seeming to create a monarchy. The lanky, plain-dressed Roger Sherman rose to remind the delegates that in his mind the nation's magistrate ought to be a servant and the representatives in the legislature his masters. They ought to have the power to remove the executive "at pleasure." George Mason calmly invoked the universal wisdom of the separation of powers to resist Sherman's argument. Reducing the executive to "a mere creature of the Legislature" would violate "the fundamental principle of good government," Mason admonished. Most of the delegates agreed, and the Convention voted against making the executive removable at the discretion of the lawmakers.[52] But the delegates also determined that the executive would not stand "above Justice." They voted that the executive could be impeached, convicted, and removed from office "for malpractice or neglect of duty" and one delegate concluded, "the Magistrate is not the King. The People are the King."[53] By September, the Convention would define impeachable offenses with greater precision to include only "treason, bribery, and other high crimes and misdemeanors." Madison, urging the necessity of precision, warned that a vague definition of impeachable offenses would be "equivalent to a tenure during the pleasure" of the legislature.[54]

So apprehensive was James Wilson that in a republic the legislature would grasp for a tyrannical degree of power that he urged the delegates to empower the executive to veto with finality any legislative act. Mason and Sherman objected that only in a monarchy could one man put a stop to the will of an entire nation. Sherman was no democrat, but his rough country manners and untutored speech revealed his humble origins. As he stood before the Convention, he looked a symbol of the very argument he was making, that in a republic "no one man could be found so far above all the rest in wisdom" as to justify an absolute veto. Mason added that it would amount to "an elective monarchy." He knew that the people would never consent. He urged that the executive be granted the power to suspend an "offensive" law until the lawmakers had "cooly" reconsidered it and either revised it or overruled the executive veto by a greater majority than was initially required to enact the measure. When the question came to a vote, the absolute veto was defeated but the suspending veto, which could be overruled by the legislature, won approval.[55] In designing the veto, the Convention deliberately departed from the British model in which the monarch, at least in theory, participated in the lawmaking process as an equal of the House of Commons and the House of Lords. The American head of state was entitled only to restrain the lawmaking process, not to resist the deliberate and well-considered decisions of the two houses of the legislature. Pierce Butler later recalled that "we had before us all the Ancient and modern Constitutions on record," and admired the British system the most. But the Convention devised an executive that was materially different from monarchy and was, he confessed, an "experiment."[56]

Once the Convention had firmly rejected the possibility of an absolute executive veto, Wilson threw his support behind Madison's proposal for a council of revision as an important way to strengthen the veto power. Join a number of the Supreme Court justices with the executive to wield the veto with greater weight and wisdom, they urged. Wilson argued that the expectation that judges would declare an unconstitutional law void was an insufficient obstacle to bad government. "Laws may be unjust, may be unwise, may be dangerous, may be destructive," Wilson predicted, "and yet not be so unconstitutional as to justify the Judges in refusing to give them effect. Let them have a share in the Revisionary power [to counteract] . . . the improper views of the Legislature." George Mason was troubled too that judicial review would not go far enough to promote good government. Judges, in their judicial capacity, would "impede, in one case only the operation of the laws. They could declare an unconstitutional law void. But with regard to every law however unjust or pernicious, which did not come plainly under this description, they would be under the necessity as Judges to give it free course," Mason lamented. "He wished the further use to be made of the Judges, of giving aid in preventing every improper law."[57]

New Yorkers had included this device for good government in their state constitution a decade earlier, empowering their governor, chancellor, and state supreme court judges to exercise a limited veto against all bills they considered "inconsistent" with the "public good." Despite the New York example and the determined appeals of Madison, Wilson, and Mason, the Convention defeated the proposal for a council of revision.[58] A majority of the delegates refused to blur the distinction between questions of constitutionality, which belonged to the judges as expositors of the law, and issues of policy and justice, which were the province of the legislators. Elbridge Gerry expressed the concerns of most of the delegates when he warned that

judges were not especially suited to deciding questions of policy. The proposed council made "Statesmen of the Judges," who lacked the "proper skill" for that role. "A knowledge of mankind, and of Legislative affairs" could not be presumed of men on the bench, said Luther Martin, and it was doubtful that they possessed the confidence of the people. The Convention believed it was imperative, Hamilton would later report in *The Federalist* No. 73, to keep the judges removed "from every other avocation than that of expounding the laws."[59]

Today, the framers' distinction between the duty of the judge and the domain of the congressman has been blurred. Judicial activists call upon the court to act as the heroic branch of government, promoting good government and a just society when the democratic process fails to mandate it. Many judges and most legal academicians insist that the court's duty extends to rectifying the incompleteness of our written constitutional guarantees, compensating for the insurmountable difficulty of amending the Constitution, and interpreting the deeply held moral convictions of the people when legislative bodies fail to express those convictions. The framers would be surprised by our dependence on the courts for good government and moral leadership. They apprehended that the nation was too committed to the principle of government by consent to invest an unelected judiciary with broad discretionary authority.

Making the People Sovereign

The delegates probed the first principles of government again when they considered how to invest the new plan of government with the status of higher law, making it supreme over the laws of the states and the acts of the national legislature. The sovereignty of the people, stated the Declaration of Independence, was self-evident. It was the people's right to invent their own form of government and define its powers. In the decade after the Declaration, Americans had learned, through trial and error, how to implement the theory of popular sovereignty. As a theory, it was well known to Europeans and Americans alike. But in 1776, almost no one understood what special procedures would make a written constitution the fundamental expression of the people's will and render it unalterable by mere legislative acts.

In 1776 and 1777, ten of the newly independent states had written constitutions. In nine of these states, the ordinary legislature drafted and proclaimed the constitution and then returned to its other lawmaking business. Although Pennsylvania elected a special convention to write a constitution, the convention did not formally submit the plan to the people for their approval. Only a few critics of these earliest experiments in constitutional government recognized that a constitution written and approved by the legislature could not limit legislative power in any practical sense. Thomas Jefferson complained without effect that the Virginia constitution of 1776 could be repealed or superseded by another act of the Virginia legislature at any time. In the next decade, Americans gradually spoke out against their state legislatures tampering with fundamental law. The people of Massachusetts insisted that "a Constitution alterable by the . . . legislature is no security at all." The Massachusetts legislators issued a call for a special convention to be elected for the sole and

express purpose of preparing a plan of government and submitting it to the towns for their approval. It was in this 1780 constitution that the phrase "We the people" was used for the first time.[60]

Building on the achievements in Massachusetts, the delegates at Philadelphia devised America's unique contribution to the history of self-government, the special ratifying and amending procedures that made the theory of popular sovereignty a reality. On June 5 and again in July, the delegates debated whether to submit the new constitution to popularly elected ratifying conventions, as Madison proposed, or to the ordinary state legislatures. George Mason called special conventions one of the most important features of the Virginia Plan. A constitution approved by the state legislatures and alterable by them at any time would stand on a "weak and tottering foundation." It was a doctrine of "great moment," which ought to be cherished as the basis of free government, said Mason, that the power to create and alter governments belonged only to the people. Madison urged the Convention to consider the distinction "between a system founded on the Legislatures only and one founded on the people." It was "the true difference between a league or treaty, and a Constitution." A plan ratified by the legislatures would, at best, impose moral limits on what government could do. This had been a principal defect of the Articles of Confederation. A constitution established by the people would become the highest law of the land enforceable by judges, who would declare any law violating it "null and void."[61]

There were also practical considerations that made it prudent to call special state conventions. Would the new plan of government be carried as easily through a two-

John Trumbull. *Alexander Hamilton*, after 1840. Oil on canvas. Gift of Thomas J. Bryan. 1867.305.

As soon as the Constitutional Convention unveiled the new plan of government, Alexander Hamilton hurried home to wage a long, arduous battle for ratification in New York State. There Governor George Clinton was already mounting a formidable campaign against the Constitution. Hamilton and John Jay recruited James Madison to join them in writing eighty-five essays in defense of the Constitution under the pseudonym "Publius." This amazing literary effort, conceived in crisis and scribbled in haste, became the enduring, authoritative treatise on the Constitution.

In *Federalist* No. 78, Hamilton rebutted the Antifederalists' claim that judicial review would give the judges an arbitrary, uncontrollable power. It was the court's duty to strike down any law that conflicted with the Constitution, which was the fundamental expression of "the intention of the people." Hamilton insisted that judges would not have the authority to substitute "their own pleasure" for the decisions made by the legislators.

house legislature as through a single ratifying convention? Would the state lawmakers readily approve a plan that caused them to lose power to a central government? Edmund Randolph predicted that jealous state politicians would spare no effort to defeat it.[62] But other delegates, especially the New England men, saw equal danger in popular conventions. Remembering the violent public meetings at the time of Shays' Rebellion, Connecticut's Oliver Ellsworth confessed that "he did not like conventions." He thought "they were better fitted to pull down than to build up Constitutions." Elbridge Gerry of Massachusetts warned that New Englanders "had the wildest ideas of Government in the world." Despite these concerns, the Convention voted for popularly elected ratifying conventions, to ensure that the new Constitution embodied the will of the sovereign people. Reflecting on the majority's decision, Oliver Ellsworth observed that "a new sett of ideas" had "crept in since the articles of Confederation were established. Conventions of the people, or with power derived expressly from the people, were not then thought of. The Legislatures were [formerly] considered competent."[63]

The following winter Madison and Hamilton would boast of this accomplishment in *The Federalist*. "The important distinction so well understood in America" between a constitution and an ordinary law "seems to have been little understood and less observed in any other country." Madison made the point that even in Great Britain where constitutional rights were talked of most, Parliament was sovereign and had "in several instances, actually changed, by legislative acts, some of the most fundamental articles of government." In America, the Constitution rested on the direct consent of the people. The stream of national power flowed "immediately from that pure, original fountain."[64] It was this accomplishment that enabled Hamilton to confidently define and justify the review power of the judiciary entirely in terms of the greater authority of the written Constitution over laws made by a legislature. It was the duty of the courts to prefer the higher law of the Constitution to mere statute law, "the intention of the people to the intention of their agents" in the legislature. Nor did this conclusion "by any means suppose a superiority of the judicial to the legislative power." It only supposed "that the power of the people is superior to both."[65]

"June 6. Very Rainy. In Convention," William Samuel Johnson entered in his diary. General Washington called the assembly to order, and the delegates again wrestled with the Virginia resolutions. On May 31, they had approved, without debate, the second resolution, that the national legislature "consist of two branches." Every state, except Georgia and Pennsylvania, had a bicameral legislature. The need for two houses to check each other, reflected one delegate, was a settled point in "the minds of the people of America." That day, the delegates had also decided that the members of the lower house of the legislature would be elected directly by the people, and on June 6 they acceded to a request from Charles Pinckney to reconsider the decision.[66]

Elbridge Gerry, trembling with the memory of Shays' Rebellion, confessed that he had little trust in ordinary men. "The evils we experience flow from the excess of democracy." In Massachusetts, it had been "fully confirmed by experience." Roger Sherman of Connecticut urged that the state legislatures choose the nation's legislators. The people had too little information and were easily misled by demagogues. Charles Pinckney's imposing older cousin, General Charles Cotesworth Pinckney, rose in agreement. "A majority of the people of South Carolina were notoriously for paper money," he said, but the state legislature had resisted their intemperate demands.[67]

The Madisonians listened impatiently and then reminded the distrusting few that "no government could long subsist without the confidence of the people." Virginia's George Mason reasoned aloud that a national government capable of acting directly on the people had to be chosen by the people. The lower house of the legislature was intended to be the "grand depository of that principle." A strong government was desired, James Wilson declared, but "its authority had to flow from the legitimate source of all authority," the people. He envisioned a federal pyramid, with the lower house of the legislature providing the broad base. Popular election of at least one house of the legislature was essential to a free government, insisted Madison.[68] But the worst ills of popular government could be cured by a carefully crafted system of representation that "refined" the public's views. The vastness and diversity of the nation made such a system possible.

Madison seized the occasion to explain why better men would be elected to the national legislature and produce better laws than in the states. He outlined the theory that he would elaborate several months later in the most enduring and often quoted piece of literature from the founding period, *The Federalist* No. 10. The mortal disease afflicting the state governments was the politics of self-interest. Each legislator was sent to represent the narrow concerns of the class, commercial interest, or religious sect in the district that elected

him. The enormity of the American republic offered great promise, Madison announced, that even in a popularly elected lower house, disinterested statesmanship in the national interest would prevail over self-interest. Political thinkers from Aristotle to Montesquieu had preached that representative self-government was not possible over a great territory whose distant borders could only be reached by the powerful hand of a monarch or despot. To such thinkers, an American republic would have been unthinkable. All of England could have fit inside the boundaries of the single state of New York. Madison argued against this common wisdom.

Countering the fears of "democracy" expressed that morning, Madison offered the vastness of the nation as a twofold cure for the injustices committed by popularly elected legislatures. In elections for national representatives, the election districts would be far larger than the districts for state representatives. If five hundred voters chose a state representative, five thousand or more would elect a national representative. Larger districts would take in a greater variety of local circumstances and interests and make it improbable that the representative elected would be attached to any interest except that of the public good. The very purpose of representation, Madison believed, was to "refine and enlarge" the views of the voters by passing them through a person chosen for his wisdom and disinterestedness who was least likely to sacrifice the public good to local or partial considerations. Just as a republic, that is, a representative government, was superior to a direct democracy in controlling the baneful effects of faction, so a large republic was even more advantageous than a small one. Whenever self-interest did find its way into the national legislature, so

Francis Guy. *Tontine Coffee House, N.Y.C.*, ca. 1797 or 1803–4. Oil on canvas. 1907.32.

The nation's first capital was a busy seaport. Francis Guy depicted the lively pace of commercial activity at the intersection of Wall and Water streets, a few blocks from Federal Hall.

many causes and parties would be brought together from the far reaches of the diverse nation that a majority was not likely to unite on any common principle but the public good. The advantage of a large republic was not in the multiplicity of its interests per se but rather in the public-spirited statesmanship for the common good that would emerge above the futile clashing of interest groups.[69]

When the vote was taken, the Convention confirmed its earlier decision that the members of the lower house would be popularly elected.[70] Despite the perils of democracy that Gerry and Sherman had recited and every other delegate dreaded, the new government had to derive its author-

ity from the people. Representation and the size of the republic, Madison promised, would mitigate these ills. It was hoped that the actual making of the laws would be entrusted to leaders who were wise enough to know the true interests of the country and patriotic enough to ignore all other considerations. The "aim of every political society," Madison would write in *The Federalist* No. 57, was "to obtain for rulers men who possess most wisdom to discern, and the most virtue to pursue, the common good of society."[71] Madison's vision of the representative as a statesman governing in the national interest has always appeared noble to many people and undemocratic to many others who want their congressman to advocate their ideas and interests. Whether a lawmaker's duty is to his own constituents or the entire nation is a tension inherent in representative government.

The Virginia Plan called for the members of the upper house of the legislature to be chosen by the lower house from a list of nominees provided by the state legislatures. Madison explained that he envisioned a small, deliberative body that would make decisions with "coolness" and "wisdom." The complex, indirect method of electing its members would shield them from public passions and interest group politics. He wanted to "refine" the people's choice through "successive filtrations." Randolph hoped that the upper house would check the "turbulence and follies" of democracy.[72]

James Wilson immediately objected that both houses of the legislature ought to be chosen by the people. To ensure that the upper house was small and dispassionate he would make the election districts very large, as great as two or more of the smaller states. John Dickinson favored a house modeled after the British Constitution. "He wished the Senate to consist of the most distinguished characters," conspicuous for "their rank in life and their weight of property, and bearing as strong a likeness to the British House of Lords as possible." Wilson shot back that "the British Governmt. cannot be our model. . . . Our manners, our laws, the abolition of entails and primogeniture, the whole genius of the people, are opposed to it."[73]

The Connecticut delegates insisted that the Convention think practically. State politicians would resent losing power and importance to national leaders. The cooperation of the state governments was vital to the union, and the Virginia Plan would not accomplish this. Give the states a role in appointing the national government, and they will support the system. The Connecticut men were waiting anxiously for the time when each state's share of influence in the legislature would be debated again. Let every state legislature select one member of the upper house, they urged.[74]

Allowing each state an equal voice was patently "unjust," objected Madison, and inviting the participation of the state legislatures ignored the reason the delegates had come to Philadelphia. "The great evils complained of were that the State Legislatures run into schemes of paper money" and other foolish measures. Delaware's George Read also rejected the wisdom of the Connecticut men. Though Delaware shared Connecticut's practical concern that every state retain its equal voice in the government, Read was a zealous nationalist. There was too much talk of what the state governments would say. "We must look beyond their continuance," he said. "A national Govt. must soon of necessity swallow all of them up." The Connecticut men bridled at Read's suggestion. They warned that if the Convention was so distrustful of the state legislatures, the states would be equally suspicious of the new national plan. "If I return to my state and tell them, we made such and such regulations for a general government, because we dared not trust you with any extensive powers," admonished Oliver Ellsworth, "will they be satisfied? nay, will they adopt your government? and let it ever be remembered, that without their approbation your government is nothing more than a rope of sand."[75] John Dickinson saw that allowing the people to choose one house and the state governments the other was "as politic as it was unavoidable." Dickinson and Ellsworth were mindful of the state attachments and interests that had to be considered. On June 7, the Convention heeded their practical appeals and voted unanimously that the state legislatures choose the members of the upper house.[76]

"Give N. Jersey an equal vote, and she will dismiss her scruples"

If the supporters of the Virginia Plan hoped that this concession would quiet all opposition to their system, they were mistaken. The small state men were ready to consider an even more divisive question: whether representation in the two houses would be granted to every state equally or according to population and wealth. On June 9, New Jersey's William Paterson, impatient under the aggressive leadership of the Virginians, raised the issue of representation. Paterson was a short, plain-featured man with a usually formal, restrained manner. But in the angriest speech heard since the opening day, Paterson raged that New Jersey would "never confederate on the plan" before the Convention. New Jersey had fewer than 150,000 inhabitants, less than half the population of Pennsylvania, Massachusetts, or Virginia. The state "would be swallowed up." He pledged that he would vote against the plan and "on his return home do everything in his power to defeat it there."[77]

The Madisonians ignored Paterson's warning. On June 11, they mustered a majority of seven states to adopt proportional representation in the lower house. Wilson threatened that if the small states found the plan unacceptable, the larger ones—a minority of the states but a majority of the people—would form a union of their own.

North Carolina, South Carolina, and Georgia, though sparsely populated, cast their votes for proportional representation, hoping and expecting that their vast empty lands would fill up quickly with free whites and slave labor. To secure this alliance between the Southern states and the big three, Wilson and the younger Pinckney moved that "three fifths of all other persons," meaning slaves, be added to the tally of white inhabitants in each state to determine representation. This "federal ratio" was so familiar to the delegates that it aroused almost no comment. It had been in use since 1783, when Congress had first adopted it to figure each state's share of national expenses. The motion was passed, with only New Jersey and Delaware dissenting.[78]

The Connecticut delegates cast an affirmative vote for proportional representation in the lower house, hoping that their action would set a precedent for compromise. They proposed that the decision just made on the lower house be combined with an equality of states in the upper house, a remedy that they would raise time and again as a meeting ground between the adamant Virginians and the recalcitrant New Jerseyites.[79] But the advocates of the Virginia Plan rejected any compromise. Before the day ended, the Convention voted six to five to establish proportional representation in the upper house.[80] Connecticut, New York, New Jersey, Maryland, and Delaware opposed the decision. Despite Paterson's angry warnings, none of the small state delegates left their seats after their defeat. It was a promising sign that the Convention would not break up before the task was completed.

Two days later, the Convention agreed to review the proposals framed thus far. Despite the bitter dispute over representation, the delegates had drafted nineteen resolutions that were a confirmation and extension of the Virginia Plan. These included a national government with an executive and a judiciary, a two-house legislature, direct popular election of the lower house and election of the upper house by the state legislatures, and most important, a broad statement of the government's lawmaking powers to include all cases in which the states were "incompetent" and to negate any state law that "in the opinion of the national legislature" conflicted with the Constitution or a national treaty.[81] The resolutions also provided for proportional representation in both houses, as voted upon two days earlier, and once again William Paterson raised the opposition. On June 14, Paterson moved that the Convention postpone consideration of the Virginia resolutions in order to hear the New Jersey Plan, "one purely federal."[82] With uncharacteristic self-restraint Madison urged the Convention to give his critics a full hearing.

The following morning, Paterson read aloud the New Jersey Plan. It was a hastily constructed standard to which the men of the small states could rally. Theirs was an uncomfortable alliance between stalwart antinationalists who saw the states being annihilated by a powerful central government and firm nationalists who dreaded that their constituents would never approve any plan reducing their state's voting power in the Congress. Among the antinationalists were Robert Yates and John Lansing of New York and the outspoken Luther Martin, who joined the alliance to the disgust of his ardently nationalist fellow Marylander, Daniel Carroll. The Delaware and Connecticut delegates also conferred on the New Jersey Plan.[83] Like the New Jersey men, they had consistently supported measures for a national govern-

ment with sufficient powers, but they were determined to preserve equal representation for the small and large states in at least one house of the legislature. They were driven to consort with Lansing, Yates, and Martin in a desperate effort to halt the momentum of James Madison and his supporters. Again and again the zealous Madisonians exhorted the Convention to adopt a "perfect system," or what "may be best in itself," without troubling over what the people expected. On June 9, Paterson had urged in vain that the delegates consider the people's wishes. Now he reminded the Convention again that "our object is not such a Government as may be best in itself but what our Constituents will approve."[84] Dickinson of Delaware told Madison privately, "You see the consequence of pushing things too far. Some of the members from the small States wish for two branches in the General Legislature, and are friends to a good National Government; but we would sooner submit to a foreign power, than submit to be deprived" of an equal vote in the legislature and "be thrown under the domination of the large states."[85]

The New Jersey Plan proposed that the Articles of Confederation be "revised, corrected & enlarged" rather than cast away entirely. The existing unicameral Congress, still meeting at New York, was to be given new powers to regulate commerce and to raise money through import duties, postage, and stamp taxes on paper items and to collect taxes directly from the citizens of any state that failed to meet its requisition. The only other important changes in the Articles were the provisions for an executive branch and a supreme judiciary. The Plan declared Acts of Congress the "supreme law" in every state and bound state judges to enforce them.[86]

The Madisonians listened patiently then

tore into the New Jersey Plan, attacking its weaknesses and inconsistencies during the next three days of debate. James Wilson reminded the Convention that legislative tyranny could only be restrained by dividing the legislature into two separate bodies. "In a single house," such as the New Jersey Plan provided, there was no check "but the inadequate one, of the virtue & good sense" of the members.[87] The plan, Madison charged, offered no remedy for one of the gravest maladies of the political system, the steady increase in unjust, unpredictable state laws.[88] Wilson insisted that under the New Jersey Plan Congress was given only a few additional powers, not the essential authority to legislate on all matters where the states were incompetent.[89] Madison objected that the New Jersey Plan was to be ratified by the state legislatures instead of the people. A constitution approved by state legislatures would not be superior to the laws of the states.[90]

In the midst of this raging debate, Alexander Hamilton took the floor on the morning of the eighteenth and held his colleagues spellbound and fascinated for five hours as he laid out his own plan for good government. His physical stature was slight, and his face was particularly boyish, fair, and delicate. But his raw intelligence and unhalting, passionate oratory held the attention of every man in the room. He was opposed to both the plans before the Convention but especially to that of New Jersey which offered no cure for the fatal disease of the Confederation. The states pursued interests adverse to those of the nation. The general government had to "swallow up" the states or be swallowed by them. Two sovereignties could not exist in one system. Hamilton proposed a bicameral national legislature empowered to pass "all laws whatsoever" and to appoint the governor of each state, who would

have an unlimited power to veto any law about to be passed in the state. He also admonished his colleagues to "go as far to attain stability and permanency, as republican principles would admit." His plan called for a national executive and a senate appointed for life. Shorter terms would not afford rulers enough independence to resist "the amazing violence & turbulence of the Democratic spirit."[91]

The speech shocked the Convention. It "would not bear discussion," recalled one delegate.[92] Fifteen years later, Hamilton denied that he had sincerely favored an executive and senate for life.[93] They were experimental propositions thrown out for discussion. Yet his other political writings suggest that the speech was true to his beliefs. Why Hamilton decided to intrude into the contest between the New Jersey and Virginia Plans with a scheme so predictably unacceptable, even unspeakable, to the majority has puzzled historians. On the battlefield, in the courtroom, and in love affairs as well, the young soldier lawyer was known to be daring, even foolhardy. They called him Little Mars. One sympathetic biographer faulted him for his megalomania. Another biographer called his speech "indiscreet and utterly pointless." It is possible that Hamilton had sat in silence too long, outnumbered and ignored by New York's two antinationalist delegates, Yates and Lansing, and was determined to make his views known before leaving the Convention in defeat. Still another historian speculated that Hamilton's passions were in check when he occupied the Convention on the eighteenth. "One would like to imagine that Madison and Wilson had decided to let Paterson, Sherman, and the others hear the views of a 200 percent nationalist, and thus to make the Virginia Plan appear as a reasonable middle ground between two extreme positions, but . . . the evidence is entirely spectral." When the speech ended, Madison simply noted that "the House adjourned."[94] The next morning, he would confront again the very real challenge posed by the New Jersey Plan.

On June 19, Madison issued an ultimatum to the small states to consider the consequences "in case their pertinacious adherence to an inadmissible plan, should prevent the adoption of any plan." The Convention voted to reject the New Jersey Plan and resume consideration of the nineteen resolutions that followed the Virginia system. The Connecticut delegates abandoned the small state alliance and voted with the majority.[95] Perhaps they heeded Madison's stern warning. It is more likely that they were confident the grievances of New Jersey and Delaware could be met without sacrificing the weeks of labor already devoted to the Virginia resolutions. "Give N. Jersey an equal vote, and she will dismiss her scruples, and concur in the Natil. system," one delegate had observed early in the debate.[96] On the twentieth, the Connecticut men raised again a simple formula for compromise, allowing proportional representation in one house of the legislature and an equal voice for each state in the other house. Finally, the Connecticut delegates and everyone else could see that the New Jersey alliance had achieved its effect. The momentum of the Madisonians had been stopped. Though the majority cast their votes for the Virginia resolutions, all but the most intransigent nationalists had come to realize that the Virginia resolutions would have to be modified in response to the concerns of the people and the delegates who listened to them. On the morning of the twentieth, Oliver Ellsworth moved that the word "national" be dropped from the resolutions, while

Speaker's desk and lectern from the First Congress of the United States. 1958.18.

The first House of Representatives convened at Federal Hall in New York City on April 1, 1789. This desk, designed by Major Pierre Charles L'Enfant, was used by the Speaker of the House. A slant-topped lectern supported by an imperious eagle rests on the Sheraton-style desk, with its slender, reeded legs.

affirming the national structure that Madison had devised. The change, though of wording rather than substance, foreshadowed other adjustments. The motion was agreed to without debate or dissent.[97]

It was in this mood of greater caution that the Convention reconsidered the proper terms of office for legislators. On June 12, the delegates had determined that members of the lower house would serve three-year terms. Elbridge Gerry had warned against the decision. "The people of New England" would "never give up the point of annual elections." It had become a Whig maxim that "where AN-NUAL ELECTION ends, tyranny begins." Gerry had stammered that he was as much against triennial elections as he was against erecting a monarchy. And he had urged the Convention to consider what the people of the states expected. Every state except South Carolina had established annual elections.[98] In reply, Madison had admonished the delegates against letting the "opinions of the people" be their guide. The Convention "ought to consider what was right & necessary." In so large a republic a three-year term would be needed for a representative to acquire "any knowledge of the various interests" of the other states. One year, he had estimated, would be almost consumed in traveling to and from the capital.[99]

On June 12, Madison had prevailed. But on the twenty-first, the majority doubted the wisdom of his quest for a "perfect system." Even Randolph and Wilson, ardent supporters of the Virginia Plan, urged the Convention to consider what was familiar and sacred to the people. The delegates voted that elections for the lower house would be held every two years instead of every three.[100]

Five days later the Convention debated how long members of the upper house would serve. Everyone agreed that stability, firmness, and independence ought to characterize that house, but there was wide disagreement on the proper term to achieve those qualities. On the eighteenth, Hamilton had shocked the Convention with his proposals for a senate to reside during good behavior. Charles Pinckney cut off any further suggestions of that nature on the twenty-fifth, when he delivered a long, remarkably eloquent oration on the uniqueness of American people. "Among them," he began, were "fewer distinctions of fortune and less of rank than among the inhabitants of any other nation." He foresaw a future of continuing equality and increasing opportunity, "because in a new Country, possessing immense tracts of uncultivated lands . . . there will be few poor and few dependent." For such a society, the British Constitution could not be the model of proper government. The British nation contained three orders of men, the American nation only one order. Edmund Randolph urged a seven-year term and vividly reminded the other delegates of the "democratic licentiousness of the state legislatures." None of the states had tried a term longer than five years.[101]

Madison and Wilson appealed for a nine-year term. The towering Pennsylvanian suggested that the Senate would probably manage foreign affairs, though the point was undecided. A lengthy term would afford the stability and efficacy needed to deal with other nations. Madison's thoughts were on domestic matters. He alerted the delegates that the design of this upper house would "decide forever the fate of Republican Government." The danger was that the "fickleness" and "passion" of public opinion would intrude into the lower house of the legislature. An upper house was needed to check the "impetuous" councils and protect the people from the consequences of their own "transient impressions." The Virginia leader conceded to Pinckney that America legally had only one order of men. But he painted the future of the nation in unusually somber tones. He saw an increase in the proportion of the population that labored "under the hardships of life" and "secretly" longed "for a more equal distribution of its blessings." He feared "the symptoms of a leveling spirit" and urged a wise, stable upper house as one remedy.[102]

The Convention listened intently to Madison's bleak vision and then to the terse, practical warnings of the New England delegates. The low-born storekeeper from Connecticut, Roger Sherman, bristled that frequent elections "were necessary to preserve the good behavior of rulers." He thought four or six years appropriate. A longer term would render the legislators unaccountable to the people. Gerry warned that more than five years would never be adopted by the people. A majority settled on six years, with a provision for rotation to ensure that a sudden change in popular opinion would not effect a sweeping change of men and measures.[103]

Throughout the final days of June, the small state delegates steeled their courage for the coming battle over the ratio of representation in Congress. On the twenty-ninth, Madison demanded that the small states renounce the "unjust" principle of equal representation. As men, not "artificial beings" called states, were to be represented in the legislature, added Hamilton, the rule ought to be according to population.[104] The Madisonians took the first victory, winning a majority of six states in support of proportional representation in the lower house. In a firm, even-tempered manner, Ellsworth said "he was not sorry on the whole" about the vote just passed. "He hoped it would become a ground of compromise with regard to the 2d. branch." Ellsworth urged that an equality of the states be established there. If no compromise could be agreed to, "our meeting would not only be in vain but worse than in vain."[105]

The debate grew grim. James Wilson uttered again his awful threat that the largest states, with a majority of people and "just

and proper principles" on their side, would unite alone. From Gunning Bedford of Delaware came the now familiar admonition that the smaller states would never ratify a plan that so reduced their voice in the national councils. "We must like Solon make such a Governt. as the people will approve." Soon Bedford's anger broke through his stony composure, and his corpulent body trembled with rage. If the large states broke away from the Union, the small states would find some foreign ally to "take them by the hand and do them justice." He was rebuked at once. Rufus King of Massachusetts was "grieved, that such a thought had entered into the heart" of the Delaware delegate, and "even more grieved" that the rash threat "had dropped from his lips." No matter how grave the problem, said King, he would never "court relief from a foreign power." Bedford's outburst was a harrowing warning that a compromise would have to be arranged quickly, before the Convention broke apart. The small state men prayed that the New Hampshire delegation, which had not appeared yet, would hurry to Philadelphia to lend their support.[106]

When the Convention reconvened on Monday, July 2, to determine the rule of representation in the upper house, the fortuitous absence of three delegates and Abraham Baldwin's wrenching change of heart produced the most dramatic vote of the summer. As the ballots were called, Massachusetts voted against the equality of the states, and as expected, New York, New Jersey, and Delaware voted aye, Pennsylvania no. All heads were turned to the Maryland delegation, where Luther Martin sat alone. His fellow Marylander, Daniel St. Thomas Jenifer, was absent. Jenifer believed in the justice of proportional representation though Maryland did not stand to benefit, and he was also bound by a warm friendship with Washington to support the Virginia Plan. But that morning, he stayed away as the vote was called, allowing Luther Martin to cast Maryland's vote for equality. Though the evidence is scant and historians disagree about whether Jenifer's absence was intentional, we know that he walked into the East Room to take his seat just minutes later. The roll call continued: Virginia, no; North Carolina, no; South Carolina, no. As the vote stood five to five, all eyes fell on the Georgia delegation. Two of Georgia's spokesmen had just left by coach for New York, where the old Congress was about to vote on a treaty perilous to Southern interests. Remaining behind were William Houston, an unyielding large stater, and Abraham Baldwin, who had been moved to forbearance by the harrowing outbursts on June 30. Baldwin withheld his support from the large state cause, offsetting Houston's vote. Though the Convention was tied, it was a stunning victory for the small states.[107]

A grand committee was proposed—one delegate from each state—to devise a remedy. "We are now at a full stop," said Sherman, "and nobody he supposed meant that we shd. break up without doing something." Wilson and Madison resisted. "Something must be done," answered Gerry, "or we shall disappoint not only America, but the whole world." Three days later the grand committee reported their plan, which embodied the points of compromise raised many days earlier by Dickinson, Franklin, and the three Connecticut delegates. First, the lower house would seat one representative for every forty thousand inhabitants and wield exclusive authority to originate bills for taxing or spending money. Second, the upper house

would abide by the one state–one vote rule.[108] On the tenth, another grand committee apportioned sixty-five seats among thirteen states, showing enough goodwill to include obstinate Rhode Island. On this day, the antinationalists Robert Yates and John Lansing, Jr., walked out in protest, never to return.[109]

A more divisive issue than how the seats in the legislature were apportioned at the outset was how legislative power would be adjusted to reflect increases and shifts in the populations of the states and the admission of new states to the Union. On the twelfth and thirteenth, bitter words were exchanged over the three-fifths rule. Weeks earlier, Madison had insisted that the "real difference of interests" threatening the Union was not between small and large states but between North and South. Gouverneur Morris, who felt "reduced to the dilemma of doing injustice to the Southern States or to human nature," announced that the people of Pennsylvania would never consent to the three-fifths rule and the encouragement it gave to the South to indulge in the wicked importation of human beings. When Wilson conceded that his state would feel less morally offended if slaves were made only indirectly an ingredient in the rule of representation, the Convention hurriedly adopted a formula that included the three-fifths rule to determine a state's population and the share of "direct taxes" it would have to pay into the national treasury. Each state's voice in the lower house was then tied to its share of the tax burden.[110] There was considerable uncertainty about what "direct taxes" meant. (More than a century later, when the Congress enacted what it thought was a "direct tax" on income, the Supreme Court declared the tax unconstitutional and the nation responded with the

Sixteenth Amendment.) In 1787 no one anticipated, at least aloud, that for many years the nation's revenue would be derived entirely from indirect taxes on trade.[111] On July 14, 1787, the vague phrase ''direct taxation'' enabled the delegates to quiet the furor over slavery, at least temporarily.

The final element in the bargain on representation was of enduring importance because it encouraged the rapid expansion of the nation, as one nation, across the North American continent. The grand committee appointed on July 2 and other delegates had warned the Convention against applying the same formula for representation to the existing thirteen states and to future states admitted from the West. The framers expected that cheap land would lure waves of settlers from the Atlantic coast to the vast expanse between the Allegheny Mountains and the nation's territorial boundary at the Mississippi River, an area of land far larger than the original thirteen states. The Western states, it was feared, would someday outnumber the seaboard states and vote against their commercial interests. Gouverneur Morris worried that Westerners would not send enlightened men to Congress. ''The Busy haunts of men not the remote wilderness'' were ''the proper School of political talents.'' But the self-taught Roger Sherman reminded his colleagues who these rough settlers would be. ''We are providing for our posterity, for our children & our grand children, who would be as likely to be citizens of new Western states, as of the old states.''[112] The Convention decided that new states and old alike would be represented in Congress on the same terms. This decision enabled the nation to extend its republican form of government across the continent as the population hurried westward, rather than spawning dependent and degraded colonies.

On Monday morning, July 16, the delegates took their seats in the State House and approved immediately the bundle of compromises they had devised to reconcile the small and large states. Until that moment, one delegate recalled, ''we were on the verge of dissolution, scarce held together by the strength of a hair.'' Even the most recalcitrant Madisonians recognized that the bargain struck that day could not be tampered with. Resolving the acrimonious struggle over representation prepared the Convention for the more difficult task that lay ahead—to forge a union between the North and the South. The accommodation also allayed the fears of many members that the states would reject the Convention's radically new frame of government. ''Whether we shall be able to agree upon any Plan which will be acceptable to the People I cannot determine,'' William Samuel Johnson of Connecticut wrote home, ''but there appears at present many circumstances in our favour.'' Even Madison would admit in retrospect that once the dispute over representation had ended, the small states ''exceeded all others in zeal.''[113] One day after the accommodation was completed, the Convention adopted by a vote of eight to two a broad statement of the new government's authority, ''to legislate in all cases for the general interests of the Union.'' Randolph called the authority ''formidable.'' Even New Jersey voted aye. Only the South Carolina and Georgia delegates dissented, fearful that so general a definition might be construed to include a power over their region's peculiar institution.[114]

Though the fears of the small states were quieted, the Convention was not Madison's own, as it had seemed to be in the weeks before William Paterson challenged the primacy of the Virginia Plan. On July 17, the delegates cut down one of the pillars of the Plan, Resolution 6, which empowered the national legislature "to nullify all state laws" that conflicted with the nation's written constitution. On May 31, the Convention had unanimously approved the resolution. But in July, the delegates ignored Madison's appeal for a strong defense against ruinous state laws and heeded instead the warning of Gouverneur Morris that the power would disgust all the states. Such an intrusion into local affairs was unnecessary, insisted the polished Pennsylvanian and the plain-speaking Roger Sherman of Connecticut, perhaps the unlikeliest pair to join forces at the Convention. Any state law contrary to the authority of the Union would be struck down by the state courts and the national judiciary.

Madison retorted that no confidence could be put in state judges to uphold "the National authority and interests." In many states the judges depended on the legislature to appoint them annually to the bench. "In Rhode Island the Judges who refused to execute an unconstitutional law were displaced . . . by the Legislature" of the state. Madison thought it was unlikely that "ordinary men would find the means to carry their grievances against a state to the nation's highest court," and he wondered whether the states would actually obey the court's decisions. But the delegates defeated Madison's scheme by a vote of three to seven and unanimously approved a provision that became known as the supremacy clause, declaring the Constitution, laws, and treaties of the United States to be the "supreme law of the land" and binding the state judges as well to uphold them.[115] Later that summer, the Convention would agree to several express pro-

hibitions that barred the state legislatures from endangering the rights of individuals by emitting paper money, interfering with contracts, or enacting retroactive laws.[116]

Madison despaired that this decision alone would render the new plan of government a failure. Many weeks after the Convention had completed its task, he would confide to Jefferson his disappointment. "It may be said" that the courts "will keep the States within their proper limits and supply the place of a negative on their laws. The answer is that it is more convenient to prevent the passage of a law than to declare it void, after it is passed."[117] Specific constitutional prohibitions would prove gravely inadequate, Madison predicted. Where state lawmakers were disposed to violate private rights, they would devise countless expedients to circumvent the written Constitution. On June 8, Madison had tried unsuccessfully to convince the Convention that the national legislature ought to be empowered to nullify state laws not only on constitutional grounds but for any reason whatsoever. Such an indefinite check was necessary for a "perfect system." Unless the national legislature reviewed all state legislation, "unjust laws would continue to be effected in the states."[118] But most of the delegates had insisted on distinguishing between laws merely unwise or unjust and laws violating the written Constitution. By July 17, the Convention had retreated even farther from Madison's vision. Most of the delegates believed that the most they could accomplish, consistent with the principles of federalism and representative government, was to devise a practical remedy in the courts against unconstitutional laws. To ensure that the laws were just, the people of the states would have to choose their lawmakers wisely.

47

The Chief Executive—Statesman or Demagogue?

On July 17, the Convention also turned to consider again how to choose the nation's chief executive. The delegates struggled with the question. That day they empowered the national legislature to make the choice. Two days later they reversed their decision and approved the concept, first proposed by James Wilson, of a body of electors chosen expressly to elect the chief magistrate. From the twenty-fourth to the twenty-sixth, they fell into another lengthy, heated debate from which they wearily escaped by resolving again on a choice by the legislature but with no confidence that this latest decision would be final. The trouble was that an executive chosen by the lawmaking branch and dependent on it for reappointment promised to be an ineffective check against legislative tyranny. One solution was to make the executive ineligible for a second term, which would have eliminated any motive for courting the lawmakers' favor. But it was understood that ineligibility would also make the executive office less attractive to ambitious, talented men, as well as depriving the nation of an experienced leader after only one term. Another solution was to let the people choose their magistrate. Many of the delegates doubted that voters in thirteen far-flung states would be familiar with the candidates and choose wisely. Even more troublesome, the delegates from the small states and the South eyed every method of presidential selection apprehensively, worrying what degree of influence their state or region would have.

By July, James Wilson had recruited an articulate, aggressive lawyer to lead the campaign for a popularly elected executive. He was the youngest member of the Pennsylvania delegation, handsome, thirty-five-year-old Gouverneur Morris. Morris had taken his political apprenticeship in New York where, as a member of the state convention that drafted the New York constitution, he had labored with vigor and success to establish the strongest executive office found in any state government. When the Convention turned to consider again Resolution 7 of the Virginia Plan, Morris rose immediately to declare his pointed opposition to a choice by the legislature. The executive "ought to be elected by the people at large," Morris insisted. "If the people should elect, they will never fail to prefer some man of distinguished character . . . some man, if he might speak so, of continental reputation. If the legislature elect, it will be the work of intrigue . . . it will be like the election of a pope by a conclave of cardinals."[119] Roger Sherman and Hugh Williamson objected that the people could not know who were the men of exceptional talent and distinguished public service. Most voters, they predicted, would cast their ballots for a man from their own state, and the largest states would always have the honor of filling the office with one of their own statesmen. It was a reasonable objection. No one could predict that within a few years presidential candidates would be known nationally as political parties transformed the American system of government. Party organizations would choose the candidates, make them known to the nation, and bring out the voters. The founders were determined against providing for political parties in the new plan of government. They had witnessed the pernicious effects of faction and party in the British Parliament and their own state governments. Party

Beekman family coach, ca. 1770. Gift of Gerard Beekman. 1911.25.

This carriage, adorned with the coat of arms of the prominent Beekman family on the door panels, is an especially fine example of the vehicles used by wealthy, colonial New Yorkers. James Beekman purchased the coach in 1771 from a sea captain. During his residence in New York as President of the United States, George Washington frequently rode in this carriage to the Beekman estate at Turtle Bay.

loyalties, they believed, were motivated by selfish interests and personal ambition rather than a disinterested concern for the public good. Hugh Williamson told the Convention that in the present, extraordinary times the crisis of independence had elevated many talented men to national stature. He doubted that in ordinary times there would be political figures recognized throughout the thirteen states.[120]

In reply, Morris took the vastness of the country and turned it from a problem to an advantage. "An election by the people at large throughout so great an extent of country," he began, would "not be influenced by those little combinations and those momentary ties which often decide popular elections within a narrow sphere." Only a distinguished reputation for public service could earn the support of voters from so many distant places. Narrow factional interests, parochial concerns, and political intrigue could not affect so extensive an election. Morris depicted the executive as a representative of the whole nation, selected in a nationwide election and answerable to no interest but the public good.[121] It was James Madison who had first fashioned such an argument, assuring the Convention on June 6 that disinterested statesmanship was more likely in a large republic than in a small one. Morris seized upon Madison's theory to defend an election of the executive by the nation rather than the legislature. In a nationwide election, men of narrow vision and local commitments would be defeated by the candidate who had earned a continental reputation for public service.

On July 17, Morris convinced almost no one that a popular election of the national executive was possible. The Convention voted ten to zero that the executive would be chosen by the national legislature.[122] Within minutes the delegates realized that they would have to reconsider their decision or bar the executive from serving a second term in order to prevent intrigue between the legislature and an executive dependent on it for reappointment. Requiring statesmen to rotate out of office and become private citizens again in order to experience with all other men the consequences of government action and understand the interests and concerns of the governed was a fundamental tenet of eighteenth-century republican thought. Under the Articles of Confederation, congressmen were permitted to serve only three terms in any six-year period. George Mason told the Convention that rotation was "the very palladium of Civil Liberty." From Hugh Williamson came a reminder that limiting the executive to one term would keep the nation from slipping backward toward monarchy.[123]

In June, the Convention had agreed that the executive would be eligible to serve only one term. But many of the delegates were coming to realize the grave consequences of the ideal of the amateur statesman. It would create frequent changes in all the policy matters managed by the executive branch and deprive the nation of its most talented, experienced leaders. Ambitious men would be discouraged from leaving other positions in government or their lucrative private careers to fill an office so limited in duration. It would destroy the magistrate's greatest incentive to an honest, excellent performance of his duties, the prospect of reappointment. Morris warned of an even more serious danger. In moments of "pressing danger," he predicted, when the nation sensed its need for a great leader, the people might prefer the "tried abilities and established character" of a past president and disregard the authority of the Constitution. "To avoid Scylla," said Morris, "we have fallen into [Charybdis]."[124]

On the seventeenth, the Convention cast aside its earlier decision barring the executive from re-election. No one doubted what the consequence of this decision would be. The dependence of the executive on the legislature for his reappointment would make the lawmakers the masters of the executive branch. It became "the unanimous sense of the Convention that the executive should not be appointed by the Legislature, unless he be rendered in-eligible a 2nd time." On the nineteenth James Wilson "perceived with pleasure that the idea was gaining ground" of some method, direct or indirect, of election by the people.[125]

Elbridge Gerry reminded the delegates again that the people were too uninformed of the best statesmen outside their own region and would be "misled by a few designing men" in the event of a direct popular election. Finally, as the day's debate was about to end, Oliver Ellsworth stood to propose what James Wilson had suggested six weeks before, a body of electors chosen from the thirteen states for the special purpose of naming the nation's chief magistrate. The Convention welcomed the proposal with a sizable majority in its favor.[126] The electoral plan offered a national executive who was experienced, national-minded, and sufficiently independent of the legislature to resist its errors.

Yet one troubling issue threatened to upset the new electoral plan—the persistent jealously between the large and small states. Immediately James Madison alerted the Convention that they expected the principle of proportional representation to prevail in the allocation of electoral votes among the states. Hugh Williamson of North Carolina moved that the number of electors in each state conform to the number of seats allotted to that state in the lower house of Congress.[127] The uncertainty evoked by these demands quietly festered. By July 24, some small state delegates were overcome with anxiety. During the next two days, the delegates trod over the same familiar, worn ground—the disadvantages of legislative selection and the interstate jealousies that thwarted an electoral plan. Wilson and Morris did not conceal their exasperation. "Of all possible modes of appointment, that by the legislature is the worst," Morris fumed. "We seem to be entirely at a loss," sighed one of the delegates. The next morning the Convention retreated to the original provisions of the Virginia Plan, confirming that the national executive be chosen by the legislature for a seven-year term and barred from further service.[128] The vote was taken in a spirit of resignation rather than victory. In September the Convention would rely on that tested device, a committee of

the states, to guide them out of the tangled web of interstate jealousies and make the electoral system a reality.

Emerging from the lengthy, contentious debates that July was a common purpose shared by all but a few of the delegates. The executive office had to be designed to attract the best men, and a method of selection had to be devised that would consistently reward them. Alexander Hamilton would soon boast in *The Federalist* No. 68 that the electoral college system made it "a moral certainty" that candidates "preeminent for ability and virtue" and a record of public service would be preferred over ambitious politicians who flattered and inflamed the public with their rhetoric. The nationwide character of the contest would offer an advantage to public leaders who had earned continental reputations. Echoing Gouverneur Morris's defense of a popularly elected executive in a vast republic, Hamilton offered assurances that "talents for low intrigue, and the little arts of popularity may alone suffice to elevate a man . . . in a single State," but not over an entire Union. The indirect character of the electoral college method was unlikely to convulse the nation with the "tumult and disorder" that a direct contest might have occasioned.[129] Demagogues and opportunists would have no motive to wage a heated popular campaign, for in each state several intermediate electors noted for their political discernment would be commissioned to exercise their own judgment in designating the next chief magistrate. Because the executive was to be eligible for re-election, Charles Pinckney told the Convention, the office would be attractive to talented, ambitious, career statesmen, and the man who filled it would stand accountable to the voters at the end of his term.[130]

Late in July, the Convention appointed

a five-member Committee of Detail to draft a constitution. Since June 19, when the Convention put aside the New Jersey Plan, the framers had met six days a week for five weeks to debate, adjust, and in some instances radically alter their first revision of the Virginia Plan. The result—the twenty-three resolutions that they entrusted to the Committee—held far greater promise of popular approval than Madison's original scheme of government. No longer was proportional representation to prevail in both houses of the legislature. The intractable small state delegates had resisted what they knew their constituents would never accept, the domination of the nation's councils by three states. The practical Connecticut delegates had foreseen also that state politicians would jealously resist the power and importance of the new national government. They would have to be wooed into supporting it. Allowing them to choose the members of the upper house was one way to achieve this. The outspoken New Englanders Elbridge Gerry and Roger Sherman had reminded the Virginian that, at least in their part of the country, the people expected their representatives to stand accountable to their constituents more frequently than the Virginia Plan would have allowed. The Convention had also defeated Madison's council of revision and disappointed his hopes that the national legislature would have an unlimited power to nullify state laws. A majority of the framers wanted to distinguish between the role of legislators and the duty of judges. Questions of constitutionality belonged to the judges as the expositors of the law, and questions of policy, justice, and national purpose were the province of the people's elected representatives. Although sectional jealousies and the newness of the task had kept the framers

from devising a satisfactory method of choosing the nation's executive, it was plain that Madison's plan violated a principle sacred to the framers and their generation, that the powers of government must be wielded by separate hands. Finally, a prudent majority had agreed to Ellsworth's motion that the word *national* be removed from the plan. Despite their caution, however, the essential features of Madison's theory had survived the thirty days of scrutiny. The new government would comprise not only a legislature but also an executive and a judiciary, each branch capable of acting directly on the citizens of the nation rather than depending on the state governments to carry out the nation's laws. And the plan itself would derive its authority from the only legitimate source of power, the sovereign people.

The moment that the Convention agreed to appoint a Committee of Detail, South Carolina's General Charles Pinckney seized the occasion to present the demands of his region. He warned "that if the Committee should fail to insert some security to the Southern States against an emancipation of slaves, and taxes on export," he would be "bound by duty to his State" to vote against their plan.[131] The Committee would heed Pinckney's threat all too generously.

On July 26, the Convention, wearied from the many weeks of debate and the summer heat, adjourned for ten days while the Committee of Detail labored. During the recess, newspapers carried notices of the adjournment and speculation about the Committee's intent. Madison read letters from Virginia telling of the public's impatience and the apprehensions that were growing as the Convention dragged on without result. Sherman and Johnson hurried to Connecticut by stagecoach to attend to pressing business, leaving Ellsworth behind to toil. General Pinckney purchased two fine geldings from a Quaker merchant, arranged for a coach, and set off for Bethlehem, with a list of the best public houses along the way. Washington traveled west of Philadelphia with Gouverneur Morris and the Robert Morris family to enjoy the summer trout fishing.[132] He took the occasion to ride over the grounds of Valley Forge, woods and hills he would never forget. There he had quartered his ten thousand troops in the winter of 1777–78, when military victory and nationhood seemed a faint hope. There he had watched twenty-five hundred of his hungry, half-clothed soldiers die of exposure. The memory must have steeled his resolve to return to the uncertain enterprise at Philadelphia where, he knew, the fate of the nation dangled.[133]

August 6–September 17, 1787

On the morning of August 6, the members strode across the graveled yard, past the stone prison into the east chamber of the State House. Awaiting them was the seven-page, printed report of the Committee of Detail. The revised resolutions of the Virginia Plan had been transformed into a preamble and twenty-three articles, in which many terms now familiar to us appeared for the first time: President, Congress, Speaker, House of Representatives, Supreme Court, necessary and proper, general welfare, and so forth.[134] Edmund Randolph had written the first draft of the report. He had admonished the Committee, whatever changes they chose to make, to address "essential principles only" and

avoid making matters into constitutional law that ought to be accommodated to changing times and circumstances. The language, too, he said, ought to be "simple and precise."[135]

The Committee's report discarded the phrase "to legislate in all cases for the general interests of the Union" and on whatever matters the states were "separately incompetent." It was John Rutledge of South Carolina who had objected to the "vagueness" of the national legislature's authority under the Virginia Plan and had called for "an exact enumeration" of its powers on May 31.[136] As chairman of the Committee of Detail, Rutledge set his mind to achieving that goal. The Committee's report granted Congress eighteen express powers, including the authority to regulate trade and levy import taxes, and one more indefinite power to make all laws "necessary and proper" for carrying out the enumerated powers. Beyond defining legislative power, the Committee framed six explicit limitations on Congress's power, including barring the Congress from laying export duties or imposing any taxes or restrictions on the importation of slaves, and requiring that all "navigation acts" receive the assent of two-thirds of each house rather than a simple majority. The prohibition on export taxes was a novelty in government, designed to soothe Southern fears that the national government would try to enrich its treasury on the labor of the five exporting states that made their livelihood on rice, tobacco, and indigo. The rule on "navigation acts" offered comfort to the South that Congress would not easily exclude European shippers from Southern ports and throw the planters at the mercy of Northern men of commerce. Southerners feared that the power to pass navigation acts by a simple majority would enable congressmen from the eight Northern states to legislate a "ruinous monopoly" on the carrying trade.[137]

The Committee of Detail had succumbed to Pinckney's demands of July 23, in fact, with too much generosity to escape protests from the stalwart antislavery men of the North. As soon as the copies of the Committee's report were distributed, the delegates adjourned for the day to study the plan. Northern resentment festered. On August 8, when the Convention was ready to confirm proportional representation in the House of Representatives, Massachusetts delegate Rufus King and Pennsylvania's Gouverneur Morris rushed to attack the hard-won understanding that for purposes of direct taxation and representation in Congress, black slaves would be counted as three-fifths "of all other persons" to determine a state's population. "The admission of slaves," said King, "was a most grating circumstance to his mind. . . . He never could agree to let them be imported without limitation & then be represented in the Natl. legislature." King rejected the Committee's plan as unfairly biased toward Southern interests. Some six hundred thousand blacks were to be counted, which was twenty percent of the nation's total population, and nearly all of them lived in the South. "There was so much inequality & unreasonableness in all of this," he thundered, "that the people of the Northern States could never be reconciled" to it. Morris offered a motion that only "free" inhabitants be counted for purposes of representation. Discarding the three-fifths rule would have upset the entire compromise between the small and large states, which Morris and King had never approved. Morris's eyes flashed as he waved his cane and shouted righteously that "he never would concur in upholding domestic slavery. It was a nefarious institution—It was the curse of heaven on the States where it prevailed." The architects of the compromise rushed to defend it. After matter-of-factly conceding that the slave trade was "iniquitous," Roger Sherman reminded the delegates that the point of representation had been settled with "much difficulty & deliberation," and he was unwilling to see it undone. Most of the delegates agreed. Morris's motion was defeated.[138] But the sinister issue of slavery loomed darkly over the Convention, like a gathering storm before the torrent.

When the Committee of Detail took up the matter of voting rights, it had simply provided that any person qualified to vote for representatives in his own state's lower house could vote in federal elections as well.[139] Deciding which Americans would have the right to vote in federal elections compelled the delegates to examine their faith in government by the people and to consider the perils of tampering with local political practices. Voting rules varied widely from state to state. Pennsylvania, Georgia, and New Hampshire permitted all adult white men who paid taxes to vote. The other states required that voters own a certain amount of real estate, called a freehold, or assets such as a business or personal property worth a minimum amount. On average, at least four out of every five white men had enough property to vote in state elections.[140]

On August 7, when the Convention opened debate on the Committee's provision, Gouverneur Morris quickly countered that the new Constitution should limit the franchise to men having a freehold. "Give the votes to people who have no property, and they will sell them to the rich," he warned. The unpredictable John Dickinson, who had insisted two weeks

Ezra Ames. *Gouverneur Morris*, ca. 1815. Oil on canvas. Gift of Stephen Van Rensselaer. 1871.1.

On August 8, the Pennsylvania delegate Gouverneur Morris issued an angry warning to the members of the Constitutional Convention that ''he would never concur in upholding . . . slavery. It was a nefarious institution. It was the curse of heaven in the states where it prevailed.'' He would sooner tax the nation to pay ''for all the Negroes in The United States than saddle posterity'' with a Constitution that allowed slavery.

earlier that "a veneration for wealth" had no place in a republican constitution, rose to defend Morris's proposal, calling a freehold qualification one of "the best guardians of liberty." Oliver Ellsworth was always the first to worry about how the new plan would be received in the states. He quietly reminded the meeting that the right to vote was "a tender point." A federal freehold requirement might fall leniently in some states and harshly in others, where land was scarce and more divided. Few men, he said, were likely to ratify a federal constitution that disfranchised them. A freehold test would also exclude merchants and tradesmen, no matter how much money they made or taxes they paid. Madison interceded that Morris was correct to suggest that the Constitution, not the states, ought to set the voting rule for federal elections. Madison called the right of suffrage "one of the fundamental articles of republican Government," which was properly settled by constitutional law. He also confessed his own fears that one day a great majority of the people would be propertyless and combine politically to imperil "the rights of property & the public liberty." Though he would change his mind later in life, Madison favored a freehold requirement in the Constitution. John Francis Mercer, who would soon storm out of the Convention to begin organizing a protest in Maryland against the Constitution, had little faith in the multitudes. He blustered that the Constitution had many objectionable features, but none more than the people's role in electing Congress. "The people cannot know & judge" the candidates. With great effort, Franklin stood to remind the Convention who "the people" were. He invoked the memory of the common soldiers and sailors who had fought in the War for Inde-

pendence. Those captured seamen, Franklin whispered, did not "redeem themselves from misery" by "entering on board the Ships of the Enemies to their Country." No class had a monopoly on republican virtue. A majority of the delegates listened quietly to Franklin's message and immediately voted against a freehold requirement in the Constitution.[141]

The next morning, recalling Ellsworth's advice that the right to vote was a matter prudently left to the states, the Convention unanimously approved the Committee's provision that anyone entitled to vote in his state was qualified to vote in federal elections too.[142] Not until the passage of the Fifteenth Amendment in 1870 did voting rights come under the protection of the United States Constitution. Since then, Americans have come to agree with Madison that the right to vote is too fundamental to our system of self-government to be excluded from the Constitution.

On August 10, the Convention took a bolder stand against wealth as the basis of political participation when they decided not to require members of Congress to own property worth a certain amount. Such proofs of wealth were called for in nearly every state constitution. Members of the South Carolina lower house were required to own real estate worth five hundred pounds, while in Massachusetts the minimum was one hundred pounds worth of land or two hundred pounds worth of other assets. The property requirements were several times higher for the states' upper houses, which, in an Americanized adaptation of mixed government, were intended to represent and protect property interests.[143] On July 26, George Mason and Elbridge Gerry, who would later withhold their names from the finished Constitution, had argued strenuously to admit only men with landed wealth into the offices of the federal government and to exclude any person with "unsettled accounts." The Convention had rejected these arguments but had instructed the Committee of Detail to report some more general wealth requirement for members of Congress.[144]

When the Convention turned to the Committee's report on August 10, Charles Pinckney immediately resisted the Committee's proposal that each house of Congress establish whatever property qualifications it deemed "expedient" for its own members. Pinckney denied wanting an "undue aristocratic influence" in the new government, but he wished to see a provision in the Constitution that would ensure every congressman possessed enough property to be "independent and respectable." It was not proper to leave the matter in the hands of Congress. Again, Ellsworth doubted that any uniform requirement would suit land-starved New Englanders and Southern farmers alike. The discussion was silenced when Franklin announced that "some of the greatest rogues" he had ever known were also "the richest rogues." This world statesman, whose eyes always looked beyond American shores, cautioned that the Constitution would be read throughout Europe and if it betrayed "a great partiality to the rich" the "most liberal and enlightened men there" would detest it. Minutes later, Pinckney's motion that the Constitution establish a property requirement for members of Congress "was rejected by so general a 'no'" that the votes of the delegations were not counted.[145] Madison spoke out quickly against leaving to Congress the authority to regulate the qualifications of its members, as the Committee of Detail had proposed. He warned that a majority of Congress could, by a simple statute, erect a set

of rules to favor a stronger faction "and keep out the partisans of a weaker faction." The British Parliament had exploited its authority over the qualifications of its members to exclude certain religious and political parties, he recalled. The Committee of Detail's proposal was soundly defeated. One ardent defender of the Constitution would boast the following winter that although many of the states allowed only men of wealth to govern, the federal plan threw "the door wide open for the entrance of *every man* who enjoys the confidence of his fellow citizens."[146] The finished Constitution required that a legislator be twenty-five years old, a citizen of the United States for seven years, and an inhabitant of the state that elected him. Congress was given no authority to devise additional requirements, of wealth or of any other sort, to restrict its membership.

The delegates wilted in the summer heat and longed to open the shutters in the East Room. They were shut to deprive the curious bystanders of even a word of the debates, but they also deprived the toilers within of any cooling breeze. The pace of the proceedings quickened, as the delegates and the people grew anxious for the task to be completed. The determined nationalist majority defined treason against the United States and provided for its punishment; confirmed that Congress would have the authority to create a system of federal courts; and departed from all historical precedent by empowering Congress, rather than the president, to "declare war," though it was understood that the executive would have the authority "to repel sudden attacks." On August 20, the Convention granted Congress the authority to make all laws "necessary and proper" for carrying out its enumerated powers.[147] By 1788, the question of what was "necessary and proper" would raise a controversy that continues to this day. But the Convention approved the phrase with no dissent and almost no discussion.

On August 21 and 22, the debate again turned to the guarantees so critical to the Southern delegates and distressing to the men of the North. The Committee of Detail's report provided, "No tax or duty shall be laid by the Legislature on articles exported from any state." The Georgia and Virginia delegations immediately reminded the Convention how fearful they were that the Northern majorities in both houses of Congress would tax Southern exports to fill the national treasury. Madison hopelessly urged his fellow Southerners to forget local interests and "be governed by national and permanent views." James Wilson objected that to deny the national government a power to tax exports would be to "take away . . . half the regulation of trade." But most of the delegates cast their votes for accommodation, voting seven states to four to confirm the guarantee that exports would not be taxed.[148]

Tempers broke loose and angry words flew across the room when the lower South's demand for the security of slavery was considered next. The Committee of Detail's report forbade the national government from prohibiting or taxing the slave trade. In a fury, Luther Martin objected that "it was inconsistent with the principles of the Revolution and dishonorable to the American character to have such a feature in the Constitution."[149] Throughout the War for Independence, patriot clergymen and abolitionists had warned Americans that the Almighty would not grant the blessings of liberty to a nation that denied liberty to one race of men. Slavery was a national sin that would provoke the wrath of God.[150] George Mason of Virginia, the owner of two hundred slaves and a man deeply troubled by slavery, reminded the Convention that any nation perpetuating this loathsome institution would incur "the judgement of heaven." John Rutledge hurried to put an end to such moral inquiry. "Religion & humanity have nothing to do with this question," he snapped. "The true question at present is whether the South[er]n States shall or shall not be parties to the Union." The Connecticut delegates rushed to defend the guarantees that the deep South demanded and predicted that slavery was destined to fade away within a few years, no matter what the federal government did. That was nonsense to Mason, who would not be silenced. The western territories were "calling out for slaves for their new lands." Mason drew a dark vision of the effects of unfree labor on the manners of the slaveholding society. Free men would learn to "despise" work, and every master would become a "petty tyrant." The Connecticut delegates pleaded again that "the morality or wisdom of slavery" were "considerations belonging to the states."[151]

A majority of the members found this pragmatism overly distasteful, but the Convention had progressed too far and struggled through too many divisive issues to accept defeat. The framers, now practiced in the art of compromise, resorted to their tested device, a committee of delegates from every state.[152] At last, on August 29, after far less contention and wearisome debate than the compromise on representation had required, the delegates sealed the agreement. The importation of slaves would not be banned before 1808, but a tax could be imposed "at a rate not exceeding the average of the duties laid on imports."[153] A simple majority in each house could pass navigation acts binding on all the states, but no duty could be laid on exports. Northern consciences were soothed, and Southern fears were partially assuaged. The Convention had invested the national legislature with the vital power to regulate commerce, had preserved the compromise between large and small states, and most important, had hurdled the highest barrier to union.

The compromise left all of the delegates somewhat uneasy. Mason and Randolph were gravely fearful that the North would monopolize their region's shipping with rapacious greed. Luther Martin bitterly opposed the moral compromises necessary for union. He would report to the Maryland legislature shortly that the same deceptive "reasons which caused [the framers] to strike out the word 'National' . . . influenced them here to guard against the word 'slaves.' "[154] Most of the delegates swallowed the compromise because their commitment to union left them no choice. Benjamin Franklin witnessed the debates in silence. Though he was President of the Pennsylvania Society for Promoting the Abolition of Slavery, Franklin did not speak a word against the compromise or present the formal petition that his organization had intended for the Convention. Slavery, he understood, was the price of union.

The fragility of the compromise would become apparent as soon as the Convention adjourned and unveiled its plan to the nation. During the ratification controversy in the states, slavery was mentioned less often than many other issues. But how it was talked about was revealing. Transferring the regulation of the slave trade from the states to the national government, even after 1808, raised Northern expectations and heightened Southern anxieties. James Wilson defended the compromise to the Pennsylvania ratifying convention as "all that could be obtained." He was "sorry that it was no more." But, he promised, the eventual authority of Congress over the trade in humans laid "the foundation for banishing slavery." At the Virginia ratifying convention, the Antifederalist Patrick Henry warned the men of his state that the future of slavery was in the hands of Americans who had "no common interest with you."[155]

During the last week of August, the delegates hurried over the Committee of Detail's report on the judicial branch. The Committee had provided that Supreme Court justices serve "during good behavior." When John Dickinson proposed that the justices be removable by the Congress and president, Gouverneur Morris and James Wilson raised their voices firmly against this assault on judicial independence. The judges would bend with "every gust of faction" in the legislature and acquiesce in the worst errors to protect their own appointments, protested Wilson. John Rutledge added another objection, that justices at the mercy of Congress could not decide impartially between the conflicting claims of the United States and a particular state. As Hamilton later explained in *The Federalist* No. 22, what made a federal judiciary so necessary was that state judges who depended on local officials for their reappointment to office were likely to be biased by local views and prefer the interests of their state over the higher law of the Constitution. They were unfit to be umpires in the inevitable, persistent struggle for power between the states and the new federal government. Men in office, Hamilton reminded the nation, naturally deferred to the authority that determined their continuance in office. The Convention confirmed that justices would serve during good behavior, removable from office only after impeachment and conviction.[156]

Fears of Judicial Discretion

Later, on the twenty-seventh, William Samuel Johnson moved to extend the federal courts' jurisdiction to law and equity and cases "arising under this Constitution" as well as under the laws of the United States. Johnson's proposals were agreed to with hardly a word of discussion, except to confirm that the judiciary's right to expound on constitutional questions was limited to cases of a judicial nature.[157] The vague phrase "under this Constitution" was the nearest the framers would ever come to explicitly empowering federal judges to determine the constitutionality of state and national legislative acts. In September, a Committee of Style would be appointed to digest the many resolutions of the Convention into an elegant, simple document. William Samuel Johnson served on the Committee, and so did John Dickinson, who opposed the review power because he feared that the judge might become "by degree, the lawgiver." Another committee member, Gouverneur Morris, who actually wrote most of the Committee's final draft, later recounted that he kept the vague phrase "arising under this Constitution," because the words expressed his own support for judicial review and gratified the vanity of another without alarming still others.[158]

The Convention understood that judicial review required a delicate treatment. The framers had freely discussed their expectations that the judiciary would refuse to carry out unconstitutional state and federal laws. Only four of the delegates—John Mercer, Wiliam Bedford, Robert Yates, and John Dickinson—questioned whether judicial review was desirable, and they were men who frequently found themselves standing apart from the majority on important issues.[159] By the 1780s state courts in New Jersey, New York, North Carolina, and Virginia were tentatively, cautiously declining to uphold acts of the state legislatures, although their state constitutions did not expressly grant the judiciary this power. Some remedy, short of the people's right to resistance, had to be devised to make the concepts of limited government and fundamental rights a reality. But the delegates knew that in some instances the state court decisions had angered the public.

In May 1787, as the Convention opened its proceedings, the printed record of a controversial Rhode Island case, *Trevett v. Weeden* (1786), was being advertised in the Philadelphia newspapers and discussed publicly. Although Rhode Island had no written state constitution, the judges there had struck down an act of the legislature because the court deemed it contrary to ancient, unwritten principles of justice. The judges had insisted that they were "accountable only to God and their consciences." Most Rhode Islanders vehemently disagreed, and the public furor over broad, discretionary judicial decision making was enough to unseat the judges at the next election.[160] In New York, Judge James Duane was noisily denounced for his opinion in the case of *Rutgers v. Waddington*. One newspaper editorial warned that when judges deemed "the law unreasonable" and showed "greater veneration" for the "Law of Nations" and the opinions of philosophers than for "the solid statutes of the state," the judges had become the lawmakers.[161] However passionately Americans wanted their laws to reach the standard of perfect justice, entrusting the courts with the discretionary power needed to achieve that objective

Ezra Ames. *George Clinton*, 1814. Oil on canvas. Gift of George Clinton Tallmadge. 1858.84.

George Clinton built a powerful political career in New York during the revolutionary crisis. Beginning in 1777, he captured the governor's chair for seven consecutive terms, though John Jay was moved to comment that "Clinton's family and connections did not entitle him to so distinguished a preeminence." Throughout the 1780s, Governor Clinton jealously guarded state powers and resisted every attempt to enhance the authority of Congress. In 1787–88, Clinton would wield his political organization and his own pen in a mighty campaign to defeat the Constitution. Writing as "Cato," Clinton sent seven essays to New York newspapers, which would be rebuked by the penman "Caesar," in reality Alexander Hamilton.

conflicted with the nation's commitment to representative government and a separation of powers.

Men within and outside the Convention understood that judicial power was a subject, in James Monroe's words, "likely to cause heats and animosities."[162] Once the new Constitution was revealed to the nation, critics would admonish the people to beware that self-aggrandizing federal judges did not try to sit in judgment on legislative acts even when there was no apparent conflict with the text of the Constitution. A "Federal Farmer" who was troubled that the court's jurisdiction extended to law and equity warned his readers that judges ought to decide cases "according to the spirit and meaning of the Constitution," not "as their consciences, their opinion, their caprice, or their politics might dictate."[163]

It was this widespread uneasiness over the proper boundaries of judicial authority that the Convention delicately skirted and that Hamilton would be compelled to address squarely soon afterward in *The Federalist* Nos. 78 and 81. Apprehensions had been voiced, Hamilton conceded, that the review power of the Supreme Court would make it superior to the national legislature and that "the power of construing the laws according to the spirit of the Constitution [would] enable the court to mold them into whatever shape it may think proper." Hamilton countered that it was incorrect to believe that "the courts, on the pretense of repugnancy may substitute their own pleasure to the constitutional intentions of the legislature." The judges were obliged to prefer the higher law of the written Constitution over an ordinary statute but never to exercise their "will" in place of their legal judgment. Defining and delimiting judicial review entirely in terms of the people's written Constitution, Hamilton assured his readers that this power would not render the judiciary superior to the Congress. Rather it would make the authority of the people superior to both.[164] Hamilton's tidy formula—tying judges to one standard, the written Constitution—was not a naive attempt to eliminate the judge's discretion entirely. But it made the problem seem controllable. Many judges and legal scholars today have discarded that formula and expect the courts to protect "fundamental" rights and values that cannot be found in the text of the Constitution or inferred from its history.

On August 28, the delegates relied on judicial review to remedy one of the most vexing problems that had brought them together, the propensity of the state legislatures to enact a multitude of laws imperiling property and other individual rights and injuring the interests of the neighboring states. By devising the supremacy clause, the framers had already made it the duty of federal and state judges to uphold the new Constitution, including any constitutional limits on what the states could do.[165] Now the Convention determined what those limits would be. Several prohibitions forbade the state governments from negotiating with foreign nations or engaging in war. The Convention acted decisively against the flood of inflationary money by barring each state from producing paper currency or recognizing anything but legal tender in payment for debts. Even the Constitution's noisiest critics would not assail this new feature once the Constitution was unveiled. Patrick Henry, spokesman for Virginia's Antifederalists, called the deluge of state paper monies "the bane of the country." To quiet the discord between the importing states, which collected huge duties at their ports of entry, and the jealous neighboring states that collected no duties but eventually bought the imported goods, the delegates had barred any state from taxing imports.[166]

Rufus King proposed an additional guarantee, to ensure that the private contracts on which credit and commerce were built would not be altered at the whim of state lawmakers. In some states, court judgments had been set aside, foreclosures canceled, and commercial contracts and corporate charters altered by legislative majorities. The Convention voted to prohibit absolutely any interference in the legal obligation established by an existing contract.[167]

How effective the courts would be in actually enforcing the supremacy of these constitutional prohibitions against willful legislative majorities in the states was uncertain. Madison still had grave doubts about judicial remedies and predicted that the states would devise ingeniously worded laws to evade the Constitution. But explicit constitutional prohibitions were what most nationalists outside the Convention wanted and expected. The following day, the *Pennsylvania Gazette*, a pro-Constitution newspaper, boasted that commerce was at a standstill because cautious businessmen awaited national remedies: "Every enterprise, public as well as private, in the United States, seems suspended until it is known what kind of Government we are to receive from our National Convention. Trading companies and manufacturing companies suspend their voyages . . . till they see how far their commerce will be protected and promoted by a national system of commercial regulations." The moneylender hoards his currency "till he sees whether the new frame of government will deliver him from the curse . . . of paper money and tender laws."[168]

On August 30, the delegates addressed a practical question of critical importance, whether the assent of all thirteen states was required, or whether a lesser number would be sufficient, to elevate the paper plan to the nation's highest law. One delegate conscientiously reminded his colleagues that the Articles of Confederation required the consent of all thirteen states to any change in the terms of union. James Wilson sprang to his feet and angrily retorted that the nation was entitled to return to first principles, regardless of what the Articles required. "We must," he said, " . . . go to the original powers of Society in so perilous a time." Elbridge Gerry called it "indecent and pernicious" to disregard the "sober obligation" of the Articles. But Pierce Butler "revolted at the idea that one or two states should restrain the rest from consulting their safety." Nine consenting states ought to be enough. He pointed out that recalcitrant Rhode Island had not attended the Convention and was not likely to consent, nor was New York, where Lansing and Yates had already fled to organize the Constitution's critics. Even the approval of Maryland was unpredictable, at best.[169]

Such revolutionary talk about evading the formal procedures of the existing government and returning to the original authority of the people, even spoken in the name of safety, brought a mood of anxious hesitation to the East Room. It was nearly four o'clock, and the delegates adjourned. They exchanged worried glances as they walked out to Chestnut Street, pondering the radical decision that necessity appeared to demand. Madison had curbed his temper that afternoon. The next morning he could no longer listen patiently when Gerry invited defeat in deference to the formalities of a lame and contemptible government.

Madison reminded the delegates that their decision in June to submit the final plan to special state conventions, rather than to the ordinary state legislatures, had settled the issue. "The people were, in fact, the fountain of all power, and by resorting to them, all difficulties were got over. The people," he insisted, "could alter constitutions as they pleased." Many of the delegates present had labored in the East Room since May, too long to discard a fair prospect of succeeding. The assent of nine states, they determined, would put the new Constitution into effect wherever it had been ratified.[170] Minutes later, the delegates drew even closer to success when they struck out any requirement that the new plan had to receive the "approbation" of the Congress at New York before being submitted to the states. With uncharacteristic caution, Hamilton wondered about the "indecorum" of bypassing Congress. But a majority of the founders heeded Wilson's warning that it would be "worse than folly" to make the future of the new government depend on the consent of the old one.[171]

As August ended, the restless delegates longed to see their task completed. The public also grew snappish with impatience, which worried the framers. On the eighteenth, John Rutledge had remarked on the public's anticipation and persuaded his colleagues to extend their daily sessions to 4:00 P.M. rather than 3:00 P.M., so anxious were they to bring the business to an end. But after six days, the new regimen had proved too arduous.[172] Newspapers that supported the Convention readied the public to receive the new federal plan. They praised the talents of the delegates and urged the public to approve whatever plan the Federal Convention presented as the best the nation could expect. "No age or country ever saw more wisdom, patriotism, and probity united in a single assembly," announced the *Massachusetts Centinel* and the *Connecticut Courant*. "We are on the brink of a precipice," wrote one Federalist penman, who warned that without a stronger national constitution, "a federal Shays" threatened to bring more destruction "than the Shays of Massachusetts Bay." The Federalist press predicted that only interested state politicians fearful of losing their own importance, "salary and perquisite men" they were called, would oppose the new plan. Antifederalist newspapers countered that what the Convention produced ought to be examined critically, not approved blindly on the faith that great men such as Franklin and Washington could do no wrong.[173]

On August 31, the Convention appointed eleven delegates to a Committee on Postponed Matters to tackle the unsettled issues, such as the mechanics of impeachment and how the nation's capital city would be governed.[174] The thorniest problem still to be resolved was how to elect the president, which had been debated again on August 24 without success.

Inventing the Electoral College

On September 4, the Committee of Eleven presented a patchwork of clever remedies and carefully measured concessions designed to make an indirect popular method of electing the president of the United States possible. That evening, as the delegates anticipated a debate on the report, Madison wrote hopefully in his diary that an end to the Convention's work finally seemed in view. The Committee's objective, Roger Sherman and Gouverneur Mor-

C. Milbourne. *Government House, N.Y.C.*, 1797. Watercolor on paper. X.285.

Proud New Yorkers erected an elegant home for the nation's president. But soon after the building was completed in 1790, Congress voted to move the capital to Philadelphia. The house became the official residence of the Governor of New York, and in 1799, the Custom House. The building was demolished in 1815.

ris explained the next day, was to rid the executive of any dependence on the legislature and motive for intrigue and to permit a good president to be re-elected again and again. He was to serve a four-year term with no limit on the number of terms. It was proposed that in each state, presidential electors be chosen "in such a manner as its Legislature may direct." Afterward the electors would cast their ballots for two persons, one of whom had to be a resident of another state. Because the Committee did not anticipate party slates, they pro-

vided that the person receiving a majority of the votes would become president and the person awarded the next highest number would be the vice president. That provision would be changed by constitutional amendment in 1804. The Committee proposed that each state be entitled to as many electors as its total representation in Congress, counting senators and representatives. The proposal allowed electors to be chosen by the people, the state legislatures, or even the state governors, all methods that had been proposed and defended tirelessly in June and July. It was a compromise between committed nationalists such as Morris and Madison who believed that a vigorous government had to be erected on a broad base of popular participation and delegates such as Roger Sherman who dreaded popular election as a "vicious principle."[175]

The Committee also provided that in the event there was a tie or no person received a majority of the electoral votes, the Senate was to choose the president and the vice president from among the five aspirants having the most votes. Sherman took care to explain what the delegates already could see, that the large states would have the advantage in the electoral college and the small states were assured an equal vote whenever the choice of president was made by the Senate.

Despite the weary delegates' eagerness to finish the plan, they did not instantly and uncritically adopt the Committee's report. Objections were raised that the Committee had thrown "the whole appointment into the hands of the Senate." Spokesmen for the Committee tried to assure the doubting majority that with "the increasing intercourse among the people of the States," men of continental reputations would become known to all the electors, and the Senate's responsibility would be rarely exercised. But it was widely feared that too many powers had already been entrusted to the Senate to allow that body to choose the president in virtually every instance, once the revered General Washington had left office.[176] Roger Sherman listened carefully to the warnings against a too powerful Senate and offered a simple solution. Whenever the electoral college failed to choose the president, Sherman proposed, let the choice be made by the House of Representatives instead of the

Senate but allow each state one vote. When murmurs were heard that perhaps the plan still contained some defect, Alexander Hamilton reprimanded the delegates. He said he would "take any system" which promised "to save America from the dangers with which she is threatened." Sherman's motion was quickly approved by a huge majority.[177]

Once the constitution makers had freed the presidency from a slavish dependence on the legislature, they dared to invest this independent, co-equal branch of government with substantial powers. These included the authority to appoint ambassadors, justices of the Supreme Court, and other officers of the national government, with the advice and consent of the Senate, and to make treaties with foreign nations, provided two-thirds of the Senate approved. Madison felt pleased with the finished design of the executive branch. That October, he would send Jefferson a full account of the Convention's labors, explaining that the presidency occasioned more confusion and tedious negotiation than any other part of the plan of government. He had no doubts about the executive branch, and he told Jefferson that most of the delegates were satisfied. In a republic, a strong executive was indispensable to check the almost irresistible tendency of the legislature to seize power.[178] Writing as Publius, Hamilton explained to the nation that entrusting the office to a single person and providing sufficient powers and an adequate term of office would afford the strength needed. The president's selection by electors chosen directly or indirectly by the people and his eligibility for re-election ensured a "due dependence on the people."[179]

In *The Federalist* Hamilton would boast that the executive branch met with great popular approval and almost no public censure. The truth was that critics of the Constitution deplored the president's four-year term. Antifederalists insisted that annual or biennial elections were essential to preserve liberty. It was a fundamental principle of republicanism, and one that the state constitution makers had observed without exception. Hamilton retorted that the president's longer term promised to free the office from a servile obedience to every "prevailing current." Men who expected their rulers to bow to the transient opinions of popular and legislative majorities had "crude notions" of the purpose of government. Whenever the president perceived a disparity between the opinion of the people or their legislators and the true national interest, it was his duty to resist the "temporary delusion" of the majority and act for the nation's good. A four-year interval between presidential elections would permit the people to re-evaluate their opinions by "more cool and sedate reflection" and would spare a good president from the consequences of a hasty, undeserved withdrawal of popular support. A generation after the new plan of government was put into effect, a French traveler to the United States, Alexis de Tocqueville, would reflect on the founders' purpose. They intended to create "an authority which would be forced to comply with the permanent determination of the majority, but which would be able to resist its caprices and refuse its most dangerous demands."[180]

Tocqueville lamented that the founders' vision of independent statesmanship no longer prevailed. The president, Tocqueville observed, had become a perpetual candidate for office, an "easy tool in the hands of the majority." "He adopts its likings and its animosities . . . he yields to its idlest cravings, and instead of guiding it as [the founders] intended that he should do, he merely follows its bidding."[181] Tocqueville was witnessing the impact of political parties on presidential selection. By the 1830s, national political parties had transformed the election of the president into a nationwide drama. Parties chose the candidates, created the campaigns, and wooed the voters. The original purpose of the electoral college, to entrust the choice of president to the most knowledgeable members of the community, had been forgotten. Voters no longer chose a presidential elector for his greater wisdom and knowledge of political matters. They picked the elector who was firmly pledged to support their favorite candidate for president. The flamboyant, slogan-filled contests tended to reward men skilled in the popular arts rather than the science of good government. Though the national political parties, as well as radio, television, and easy means of travel, have rendered the electoral college obsolete, we can benefit from recalling the kind of presidential leadership the electoral college was designed to reward—disinterested statesmanship in the national interest.

One of the most promising signs that the people would actually ratify what the framers were devising appeared on September 10. The delegates daringly discarded the amending procedure established under the Articles of Confederation and adopted an easier procedure for changing constitutional law. Any amendment to the Articles required the consent of all thirteen states, as well as Congress. During the 1780s every attempt to enlarge the central government's powers over trade and taxation had been frustrated by one or two recalcitrant states. From the opening days of the Convention, it was agreed that the "novelty and difficulty" of inventing a new government necessitated some workable procedure for making future adjustments. Better to plan for changes made in a "regular and constitutional way than to trust to chance and violence." On the tenth, Madison offered a proposal that won the Convention's support. As soon as two-thirds of the House of Representatives and two-thirds of the Senate reached agreement on a proposed amendment, it would be presented to the state legislatures or special conventions in each state. The consent of three-fourths of the states, rather than unanimity, would be sufficient to effect the change. A few days later, the delegates adjusted Madison's proposal to allow a nationwide convention to frame amendments in the event that Congress failed to respond to the people's desire for change.[182] The simple, attainable method that the founders provided for constitutional change would be of critical importance the following winter, when the people decided whether to ratify a plan of government that they deemed imperfect and incomplete. The influential John Adams, then Minister to Great Britain, admitted that the new plan had shortcomings, especially a too powerful Senate and no bill of rights. In a second volume of his acclaimed *Defence of the Constitutions of Government of the United States of America*, which would appear at the peak of the feverish ratification controversy, Adams reminded his readers that "a people who could conceive and adopt" their own government "will be able to amend it, when by experience, its inconveniences and imperfections shall be seen and felt."[183]

Nearly five decades after the Constitution was written, Alexis de Tocqueville still praised the formal amending procedure. In *Democracy in America* (1835), he lamented

that his own nation lacked a prescribed method for altering its fundamental law. In France, no change was possible unless the legislature simply exceeded its constituted powers. In that event, the judiciary did not have the authority to stop the legislature and declare its act unconstitutional, noted Tocqueville. He deemed it a good thing. Better to concede the "power of changing the constitution of the people to men who represent [however imperfectly] the will of the people" than to judges "who represent no one but themselves." Americans were not faced with this unenviable choice between unlimited legislative power and rule by the judiciary, he observed. Neither branch of government could claim to speak for the people in a fundamental sense. America's formal amending procedure removed "any danger of this kind" by providing a procedure for legitimate constitutional change.[184] In the twentieth century, many legal scholars argue that the amending process has proved too difficult. It has become the court's duty, they say, to rectify the incompleteness of written constitutional guarantees and to "keep the Constitution adjusted to the changing needs of the time."[185] Critics of such judicial activism object that no matter how much the written Constitution may lag behind what the people believe and want, judges are not particularly qualified to understand and interpret the people's values and political ideals.[186] The more important principle, which Tocqueville understood, is that allowing any branch of government to alter the very Constitution that establishes and limits its power is to abolish constitutionalism altogether and surrender to a government of unlimited power.

The delegates hastened to complete their work. On September 8, they had appointed a five-man Committee of Style to bring in a final draft, and only four days later the Committee was ready to report.[187] Throughout the summer the Convention had made clever use of committees to accomplish tasks unsuited to a large assembly, as well as to produce accommodations when endless days of debate had yielded only rancor. The Committee of Style began its work where the Committee of Detail had left off, reducing the twenty-three articles amended and agreed to in the Convention to a spare seven. The document was extremely plain, merely describing the powers of the legislative, executive, and judicial branches and the means of choosing their officers, the prohibitions on the states, and the mechanics of ratifying and amending the plan. No salutations to the rights of man or the wisdom of separate powers compromised its austere practicality. The provisions were general enough to meet the needs of later generations, as Randolph had urged, and with the procedure for future amendments promised that the authority of the Constitution would endure as long as the ideals of the men who wrote it remained dominant. To Gouverneur Morris and James Wilson belonged most of the credit for the elegantly simple document.[188] The firm of Dunlap and Claypoole was trusted to print a copy for each of the delegates without leaking a word of the report to the anxious nation.

The most striking stylistic change was to the preamble. On August 7, the Convention had agreed to an opening phrase proposed by the Committee of Detail that read, "We the people of the states of New Hampshire, Massachusetts, Rhode-Island and Providence Plantations, Connecticut, New-York, New-Jersey, Pennsylvania, Delaware, Maryland, Virginia, North-Carolina, South-Carolina, and Georgia, do ordain and establish. . . ."[189] The Committee of Style struck out the reference to the states and began the preamble, "We the people of the United States. . . ." The change had been made necessary by the Convention's decision on August 31 that the new government should go into operation once nine states, instead of all thirteen, had ratified. No one knew which states would ratify first, or even at all. The Committee had no choice but to adopt a ringing declaration of American unity.[190]

For the next four days, September 12 to 15, the delegates perfected and polished the report. Madison later recalled that the pace of decision making quickened and speeches became shorter as fatigue, impatience, and the pressure of obligations at home overwhelmed the delegates. Yet they stopped to consider some fifty changes to the Committee's report and adopted half of them. On the twelfth, one of the North Carolina delegates proposed that the majority required to override a presidential veto be reduced from three-fourths to two-thirds of each house. The plan put too much power in the hands of the president. Madison countered that a strong presidential veto was needed to prevent the "popular or factious injustice" so commonly committed by legislatures. But a majority approved the change to two-thirds.[191] On the fourteenth, the Convention struck out a phrase in Article I, empowering the Congress to "punish offences against the law of nations." Most of the delegates thought that the unwritten standards of international conduct known as the "law of nations" were "too vague" a rule. Let Congress "define" the crimes against other nations by statute, just as piracies and felonies were defined, before providing for their punishment.[192]

WE, the People of the United States, in order to form

a more perfect union, ~~to~~ establish justice, insure domestic tranquility, provide for the common defence, promote the general welfare, and secure the blessings of liberty to ourselves and our posterity, do ordain and establish this Constitution for the United States of America.

ARTICLE I.

Sect. 1. ALL legislative powers herein granted shall be vested in a Congress of the United States, which shall consist of a Senate and House of Representatives.

Sect. 2. The House of Representatives shall be composed of members chosen every second year by the people of the several states, and the electors in each state shall have the qualifications requisite for electors of the most numerous branch of the state legislature.

No person shall be a representative who shall not have attained to the age of twenty-five years, and been seven years a citizen of the United States, and who shall not, when elected, be an inhabitant of that state in which he shall be chosen.

Representatives and direct taxes shall be apportioned among the several states which may be included within this Union, according to their respective numbers, which shall be determined by adding to the whole number of free persons, including those bound to service for a term of years, and excluding Indians not taxed, three-fifths of all other persons. The actual enumeration shall be made within three years after the first meeting of the Congress of the United States, and within every subsequent term of ten years, in such manner as they shall by law direct. The number of representatives shall not exceed one for every *thirty* thousand, but each state shall have at least one representative: and until such enumeration shall be made, the state of New-Hampshire shall be entitled to chuse three, Massachusetts eight, Rhode-Island and Providence Plantations one, Connecticut five, New-York six, New-Jersey four, Pennsylvania eight, Delaware one, Maryland six, Virginia ten, North-Carolina five, South-Carolina five, and Georgia three.

When vacancies happen in the representation from any state, the Executive authority thereof shall issue writs of election to fill such vacancies.

The House of Representatives shall choose their Speaker and other officers; and ~~they~~ shall have the sole power of impeachment.

Sect. 3. The Senate of the United States shall be composed of two senators from each state, chosen by the legislature thereof, for six years: and each senator shall have one vote.

Immediately after they shall be assembled in consequence of the first election, they shall be divided as equally as may be into three classes. The seats of the senators of the first class shall be vacated at the expiration of the second year, of the second class at the expiration of the fourth year, and of the third class at the expiration of the sixth year, so that one-third may be chosen every second year: and if vacancies happen by resignation, or otherwise, during the recess of the Legislature of any state, the Executive thereof may make temporary appointments until the next meeting of the Legislature.

No person shall be a senator who shall not have attained to the age of thirty years, and been nine years a citizen of the United States, and who shall not, when elected, be an inhabitant of that state for which he shall be chosen.

The Vice-President of the United States shall be, ~~ex officio~~, President of the senate, but shall have no vote, unless they be equally divided.

The Senate shall choose their other officers, and also a President pro tempore, in the absence of the Vice-President, or when he shall exercise the office of President of the United States.

The Senate shall have the sole power to try all impeachments. When sitting for that purpose, they shall be on *oath or affirmation.* When the President of the United States is tried, the Chief Justice shall preside: And no person shall be convicted without the concurrence of two-thirds of the members present.

Judgment in cases of impeachment shall not extend further than to removal from office, and disqualification to hold and enjoy any office of honor, trust or profit under the United States: but the party convicted shall nevertheless be liable and subject to indictment, trial, judgment and punishment, according to law.

Sect. 4. The times, places and manner of holding elections for senators and representatives, shall be prescribed in each state by the legislature thereof: but the Congress may at any time by law make or alter such regulations, *except as to the places of chusing senators.*

A Political Blunder

None of the changes and additions adopted on these final days was as important as the defeat of George Mason's proposal to draft a bill of rights. On the twelfth, Mason exhorted the delegates that such a bill would "give great quiet to the people." Mason had almost single-handedly written the Virginia Bill of Rights in 1776. "With the aid of the state declarations," he told the weary and reluctant delegates, "a bill might be prepared in a few hours." The state bills were sufficient, resisted Roger Sherman. Mason, who never hesitated to exert his own opinion against an overwhelming majority, shot back that "the laws of the U.S." were "paramount to the state bills of rights." State guarantees could not protect citizens from an overbearing federal government. Mason reasoned correctly. But the Convention voted zero to ten against writing a bill of rights, with even the Virginia delegation opposing it.[193]

Two days later, as the delegates traveled wearily over the Committee of Style's report, step by step, clause by clause, an unexpected motion was offered by Elbridge Gerry and Charles Pinckney "that the liberty of the Press should be inviolably preserved." Again Sherman answered that "it was unnecessary. The Power of Congress," he reminded, did not "extend to the Press." The Convention hastily discarded the motion, four to seven.[194] The decision ran against the hard-learned lessons of the American Revolution and would soon shock the nation.

From the Stamp Act crisis of 1765 to the outbreak of the War for Independence a decade later, the American colonists had invoked natural law, sacred rights, and ancient British custom to denounce the oppressive Acts of the Parliament of Great Britain as "unconstitutional." The Acts were not simply unjust. They were legally void. Laws of God and nature, though unwritten, were of superior legal standing to any conflicting Acts of Parliament, the Americans had insisted.[195] But the American argument had failed. The Declaration of Independence, a statement of principles and natural rights that could be defended only by revolution, symbolized that failure. Unwritten rights and principles offered no legal protection against tyrannical rulers. In the decade after Independence, Americans would struggle with the question left unanswered by the American Revolution: What kind of higher law could be made an actual, legally enforceable limit on what government could do? Americans were gripped by an enthusiasm for written constitutions, and between 1776 and 1780 eight of the states that wrote constitutions also adopted bills of rights. Whether their liberties originated in nature, God, or customary British usage, many Americans were concluding that giving these liberties the unambiguous status

OPPOSITE PAGE: A preliminary draft of the United States Constitution, September 13, 1787, with annotations by William Livingston.

On September 8, the framers appointed a Committee of Style to draft a formal plan of government based on the twenty-three resolutions they had agreed to in the Convention that summer. On September 12, the Committee finished its labors and commissioned a Philadelphia printer, who was sworn to secrecy, to prepare printed copies for the Convention's use. The next day, the printed draft of the Constitution was laid before the delegates for a final round of debate and revisions.

The document pictured here was used by one of the New Jersey delegates, William Livingston, who noted by hand the last-minute changes the Convention made on September 13–15. Late in the afternoon on Saturday, September 15, the forty-two delegates present voted on the final question to agree to the Constitution as amended.

of written, constitutional law would shield them from unjust rulers.

In September 1787, James Madison voted with the Convention majority against drafting a federal bill of rights. Its practical value would be meager, he believed. The state bills of rights had proved to be mere "parchment barriers." Madison continued to favor his proposal for a council of revision, a remedy that joined the weight of the executive with the judiciary and did not distinguish between what was unwise or unjust and what was prohibited by a written constitution.[196]

Once the new federal plan was unveiled, critics of the Constitution in every state would protest noisily that the omission of a bill of rights disappointed the people's expectations and left their liberties unsecured. How the framers defended their decision suggests what they might have been thinking on September 12 and 14, when they dismissed the need for a bill of rights with only a few words of debate. Where the powers of the general government were few and defined, no bill of rights was needed, they insisted. Throughout history, constitutions had invested the ruler with every right and authority not explicitly reserved to the people. The early state constitutions embodied this principle. The new United States Constitution established a different concept, the framers argued, that every power not delegated to the general government remained in the people's hands.[197] But the Antifederalists hammered away at this argument and denied that the powers delegated to the government were sufficiently defined and limited. Again and again they pointed to the dangers posed by a national legislature empowered to make all "necessary and proper" laws for putting its express powers into effect. It was possible, as well, that precious liberties might be tampered with even when the government did not exceed its constituted powers.[198]

In defense of the Convention's decision, Edmund Randolph called it "inconceivable" that judges "would uphold a legislative act that was contrary to justice or inflict a punishment they deemed oppressive." Theophilus Parsons promised the statesmen of Massachusetts who assembled to vote on the Constitution that a bill of rights was unnecessary because no court would enforce an Act of Congress that infringed any one of the natural rights of the people. But most Americans wanted more security for their rights than the discretion of judges or the ultimate right to revolution. A declaration of rights was necessary, Jefferson warned Madison at the height of the ratification controversy, to put the people's essential liberties "on a legal basis." The rights reserved to the people could not be allowed "to rest on inference." Some of the framers explained how troubled they had felt that any bill of rights they drafted would inevitably be incomplete. "All the political writers from Grotius and Puffendorf down to Vattell" had tried to catalogue the "rights of men in a political society," James Wilson told the Pennsylvania ratifying convention, and not one of them, not indeed all the philosophers together, had devised "a complete enumeration of rights." The danger, Wilson predicted, was that enacting a partial bill would, by implication, imperil any rights omitted. Once the security of rights depended on their being incorporated into the written Constitution, unwritten rights would have no safety or legitimacy.[199] Madison regarded this as "one of the most plausible arguments" he "ever heard against . . . a bill of rights." He also apprehended a "great reason to fear" that some liberties, such as the rights of conscience, would not be "positively declared with req-

Asher B. Durand. *John Adams*, 1835, after Gilbert Stuart. Oil on canvas. Gift of the New York Gallery of Fine Arts. 1858.6.

In December 1786, as the nation prepared for a Constitutional Convention, John Adams published the first volume of his treatise on the principles and structure of good government, *A Defence of the Constitutions of Government of the United States of America*. He began with an eloquent accolade to the authors of the state constitutions created after Independence. Governments invented "by the use of reason" and "founded on the natural authority of the people alone, without a pretense of miracle or mystery" were "a great point gained in favor of the rights of mankind."

In the third volume, which appeared in January 1788 at the height of the controversy over ratification, Adams lavishly praised the Convention "as the greatest single effort of national deliberation that the world has ever seen." The Constitution had shortcomings—no bill of rights and a too powerful Senate. But "a people who could conceive and adopt" their own government "we need not fear will be able to amend it, when by experience, its inconveniences and imperfections shall be seen and felt." What merited celebration was the act of inventing. "The world has been too long abused," wrote Adams, with notions that a particular climate or soil or a "certain celestial virtue" was necessary to liberty. The true source was "a well-ordered constitution."

uisite latitude," if submitted to the public for definition.[200]

In 1788, Madison would ask Jefferson's advice on this dilemma, and Jefferson would shrug that "half a loaf is better than no bread. If we cannot secure all our rights, let us secure what we can." Many Americans agreed with Jefferson and found the framers' reasons for omitting a bill of rights unconvincing. As the states ratified the new federal plan, nearly all of them would also issue unequivocal demands for immediate amendments to secure rights.

By the winter of 1788, the strength of the Antifederalist opposition to the new Constitution, especially in Madison's own state, convinced him that rights amendments were a political necessity. In a letter to Jefferson that winter, Madison accused the Antifederalists of exploiting the absence of a bill of rights in order to destroy public confidence in the plan. The true ground of their opposition, reported Madison, had to do with the extent of federal authority and "the articles relating to treaties, to paper money, and to contracts." The amendments the Antifederalists were proposing changed the structure and powers of the federal government rather than securing individual liberties. As soon as the new government was formed and the First Congress convened in 1789, Madison would urge his fellow legislators to propose a bill of rights immediately. Swift action would seize the initiative from the "designing advocates" of amendments who were less concerned to protect individual rights than to tear away at national power.[201]

In the summer of 1789, Madison would lay before Congress nine proposed additions to the Constitution, which became the Bill of Rights. His draft included provisions for freedom of speech, press, and as-sembly, the right to bear arms, due process of law, and protection from excessive bail, unreasonable search, or punishment without a trial by an impartial jury of neighbors. It also affirmed the separation of legislative, executive, and judicial powers and reiterated that all powers not delegated were reserved to the states or to the people. Madison took the occasion to remind the First Congress of the lesson of the American Revolution. In the mother country, where the authority of Parliament was not limited by a written constitution, even the liberties Englishmen deemed ancient and sacred could be abolished at the legislature's discretion. Common law and natural law principles offered no practical protection against legislative injustice. If our liberties "are incorporated into the Constitution," declared Madison, the courts will be their "guardian." Judges will "resist every encroachment upon rights expressly stipulated" in the federal plan.[202] The young Virginian had learned a great deal about the nation's attachment to written law as the bulwark of freedom since September 12, 1787, when he had sat in the East Room of the State House, quietly recording and acquiescing in the Convention's decision against a bill of rights.

On September 15, 1787, the Convention made the final changes to the Committee of Style's report and these carried great symbolic weight. Roger Sherman, a spokesman for the small states, and Gouverneur Morris, a firm advocate of the large state interests, together urged that a proviso be added that "no State, without its consent, shall be deprived of its equal suffrage in the Senate." The motion, which was "dictated by the circulating murmurs of the small States," was "agreed to without debate." Not even Madison dared to raise an objection, and never again would a jealousy between large and small states threaten the Union.[203] Virginia's George Mason, noting the Convention's eagerness to relieve all lingering doubts and divisions, proposed "that no law in the nature of a navigation act be passed before the year 1808, without the consent of 2/3 of each branch of the Legislature." Mason's motion won the approval of only three states, and within minutes he declared his intention to withhold his signature from the finished plan. Madison regarded his fellow Virginian's dissent as "a subject of regret," and indeed it was, for it symbolized the unassuageable Southern distrust that would one day shatter the Union.[204]

At last, every proposal had been heard, every phrase read and considered. As the moment arrived for the delegates to vote formally on the completed plan, Randolph took the floor and spoke hesitantly. Referring to the "dangerous and indefinite power" given to Congress, Randolph confessed his embarrassment that he would not put his name to the plan unless the Convention provided for a second constitutional convention. Let the people of the states offer amendments to be considered and approved at a second convention. Mason immediately followed. "It was improper to say to the people, take this or nothing." He too would withhold his signature unless the delegates consented to a second convention. Elbridge Gerry listed thirteen objections to the Constitution, dwelling on the power of Congress to make all "necessary and proper laws," and supported Randolph's motion. "Nothing but confusion" would result from the proposal, countered Charles Pinckney, who reminded the delegates that dissolving governments to create new ones was a dangerous, uncertain enterprise. "Conventions are serious things, and ought not to be re-peated." Randolph's motion was rejected by every delegation. A decision was called on the Constitution, and all the states voted aye.[205]

Forty-two delegates walked down Chestnut Street into the State House on Monday, September 17. All but three came ready to sign the parchment document that had been prepared over the weekend. As they walked out of the sunny morning air into the quiet, shaded East Room to take their seats, their faces wore a tired look. Yet many delegates smiled in amazement at the task they had completed. Benjamin Franklin, growing daily more feeble, was carried into the room in his sedan chair. He too was proud but also visibly worried that public knowledge of the doubts and disagreements that had been uttered in the room would prove fatal to the plan. The Constitution was read a final time to the delegates, who knew every phrase by heart. Franklin rose to speak but faltered and handed his prepared remarks to James Wilson to present. Franklin's gentle, forgiving appeal for accommodation must have fallen awkwardly from the lips of the headstrong, uncompromising younger delegate. The aged statesman wanted the three dissenters to forget their differences and lend their names to the finished plan. He reminded them that "when you assemble a number of men to have the advantage of their wisdom, you inevitably assemble with those men, all their prejudices, their passions, their errors of opinion, their local interests, and their selfish views." The plan was not perfect, but he was astonished to find that a work of compromise came "so near to perfection. . . . The opinions I have had of its errors . . . I have never whispered a syllable of them abroad—Within these walls they were born and here they shall die." He urged unanimity "whether real or apparent." He wished that every member who still had objections to the plan would "doubt a little of his own infallibility" and put his name to the instrument.[206]

Nathaniel Gorham of Massachusetts suddenly offered the thought that "if it was not too late," the Convention ought to increase the size of the House of Representatives by providing one representative for every thirty thousand inhabitants, rather than for every forty thousand. The change would alleviate concerns about the adequacy of representation in the national Congress, said Gorham, who neglected to add that it would also favor the large states at the expense of the small ones. The power of Washington's presence was immediately felt. For four months he had refrained from offering his sentiments on any point of controversy, but "he could not forbear expressing his wish that the proposed alteration might take place." The motion was approved without delay or a murmur of dissent from the small states.[207]

Edmund Randolph rose next and apologized for his steadfast decision against signing. Gouverneur Morris confessed that "he too had objections," but he saw "general anarchy" as the only alternative to the present proposal. Alexander Hamilton predicted that even one missing signature might do "infinite" harm. Franklin spoke again, "professing a high sense of obligation to Mr. Randolph" for having proposed the initial plan on May 29 and urging him one last time to "prevent the great mischief which the refusal of his name might produce."[208] But Randolph held firmly to his decision and stood aside with Mason and Gerry as the other delegates walked forward to sign the United States Constitution.[209]

The last decision that the framers made was probably unwise. Rufus King suggested that the official journal of the debates be either destroyed or held in secrecy by the president of the Convention. King worried that critics of the Constitution would make "bad use" of the records to prevent its adoption.[210] Like declining to draft a bill of rights, this decision against disclosing the Convention's deliberations as soon as the Constitution was unveiled carelessly overlooked what the nation had come to expect as a matter of right. The secrecy rule adopted on May 29 had aroused very little criticism that summer. Luther Martin, who found nearly every decision of the Convention objectionable, complained about secrecy too. One congressman of New York quietly deplored it as contrary to the principles of representative government. But all summer long the rule was hardly mentioned publicly, and on those rare occasions the newspapers treated it approvingly. Secrecy had heightened the people's impatience and allowed speculative rumors to fly through the states that the framers intended to exclude Rhode Island from the Union or send to Europe for a king. However, the advantages of the secrecy rule had been great, enabling the delegates to consider far bolder proposals for change than a prudent concern for public opinion and their own political careers would have permitted. Americans expected that once the Convention had adjourned, the rule of secrecy would be lifted. "No pains shall be spared to procure the debates and resolutions of the Convention for the inspection of the public," announced one New York newspaper with great anticipation. The Convention's final, unexpected decision gave the Antifederalists a solid pretext to accuse the drafters of drawing a "thick veil of secrecy" over their meeting and conspiring to establish an aristocratic form of government.[211]

Sixteen of the delegates did not appear at the State House on the final day. Typical was Oliver Ellsworth, who had hurried back to his duties on Connecticut's Supreme Court at the end of August. Only four of those absent had left the Convention in protest. John Lansing, Jr., and Robert Yates had rushed home to organize the opposition to the Constitution in their state, leaving only Alexander Hamilton to sign for New York. Luther Martin and John Francis Mercer of Maryland had also stormed out. The framers did not despair over the dissent of the few, despite the ominous tone of Franklin's warning. They marveled at the accomplishment of the majority. Madison called the Convention's achievement a "real wonder." He had grave misgivings, particularly that representation in the Senate was unjust and that federal courts would be unable to resist the viciousness of the state legislatures. Yet he confessed that it was "impossible for any man of candour to reflect" on what had been accomplished "without partaking of the astonishment."[212]

The fear of impending national ruin drove the majority to pursue success, even when irreconcilable differences or sheer fatigue seemed about to prevail. If they failed, Hamilton typically warned them, "anarchy and confusion" would be the result. But more than fear, what inspired the delegates to persevere was their self-awareness that they had been given a task of historic importance. This generation and this nation were destined, declared Hamilton, "to decide the important question, whether societies of men are really capable or not of establishing good government from reflection and choice" or must forever succumb to fate and force.[213] Also critical to the framers' success was their shared commitment to representative self-government and their determination to mitigate its worst dangers. No proposal was seriously considered that did not provide for executive and legislative leaders elected frequently by the people, either directly or indirectly. The delegates declined to formulate any federal restrictions on who could vote and boldly discarded the property qualifications found in the state constitutions that allowed only the wealthy to serve in government. The delegates were, nevertheless, apprehensive of the evils of unfettered majority rule.

By September 17, checks were in place to ensure that laws would not be made by a simple majority united by some passion or interest contrary to the public good or the rights of other citizens. The Convention had devised a lengthy, complex lawmaking procedure and entrusted the execution and enforcement of the laws to separate branches of the government. But checks, if carried too far, would have produced a government of inaction, which few of the delegates, least of all such ardent nationalists as James Madison and James Wilson, desired. The best government, the delegates agreed, was not the one that governed least. "No man is a warmer advocate for proper restraints and wholesome checks for every department of Government," began Washington, but it was foolish to deprive men of the authority to "render essential services" because a possibility remained "of their doing ill."[214] Good government depended less on institutional checks and more on experienced, talented, honest leaders. The offices of government had to be designed to attract wise, public-spirited men, and an electoral system was needed that would consistently return those men to office and discourage demagogues. On no other problem did the framers labor longer and with more determination than the invention of a system to select a president, the officer who most fully embodied the opposing ideals of accountability to the electorate and independent statesmanship in the national interest.

This final session had been the longest one of the summer. It was six o'clock when the members swung open the doors of the State House for the last time and walked together to the City Tavern for a farewell dinner. Washington noted in his diary that after the convivial gathering, he retired to his room "to meditate on the momentous work which had been executed after not less than five ... and sometimes seven hours sitting every day except Sunday" for more than four months.[215] Anticipation of the enormous task ahead, to win the approval of the thirteen states, must have tempered the joyousness of the evening. Nowhere in the Constitution did the word "national" appear. Ellsworth's successful motion to drop the term was never reversed. But the new frame of government was undeniably national in structure and purpose. Throughout the summer, the del-egates had been reminded in letters from home that should the Convention "unite in their doings without attempting too much," their labors would be well received. One Connecticut politician explained to William Samuel Johnson that when the states united for the first time during the American Revolution and consented to the Articles of Confederation, they had "the strong impression of Fear" to forge the Union. But in peacetime rather than war, Americans would be "cautious" how they gave power to their rulers, would "deliberate with Coolness & Circumspection & with great Reluctance alter their old forms of Government."[216] The delegates had worked pragmatically to devise a government acceptable to the people. Yet the end product was a radical departure from the principles of Confederation and from the mandates of the delegates. It was a testimony to the bold belief of its authors that not only a small, homogeneous country but even a vast republic embracing many diverse interests could be governed as one nation.

The Founders' Prescription
for Good Government

MOST Americans credit the nation's founders with checks and balances, the separation of powers, and the Bill of Rights. All these are constitutional devices to stop government or slow it down whenever power is about to be abused or individual liberties are in danger. But to the authors of the Constitution, these were measures of last resort should the system fail to work as they hoped it would. The essence of their plan, though almost forgotten today, was a theory of leadership. The framers wanted to make the chief offices of the national government attractive enough that talented, ambitious men would be lured from more lucrative private careers. And they intended to design an electoral system that would consistently reward the most able, virtuous men and give them the independence to rule wisely.

Who was entitled to vote was a state matter, which the Constitutional Convention prudently refused to tamper with, neither depriving nor guaranteeing the right to anyone. But the founders made practical decisions about the tenure, size and method of choosing each house that determined what the actual relationship between the voters and their representatives would be. The Antifederalists charged that the constitution makers intended to tear the privilege of self-government away from the people by making their representatives too independent and unaccountable. A candid examination of the debates and literature from the period suggests that the Federalists' motive was quite different. They wanted to devise a system of representation that would encourage national greatness because it elevated the common good above the clashing interests of different classes, religious sects, and geographic

Joseph Wright. *John Jay*, 1786. Oil on canvas. Gift of John Pintard. 1817.5.

John Jay ardently supported the movement for a stronger central government. Because New York politics was dominated by the antinationalist Governor George Clinton and his followers, Jay was not named to the delegation that went to Philadelphia in 1787. He campaigned tirelessly for ratification, writing pamphlets, attending the state convention at Poughkeepsie, and contributing five essays to *The Federalist*.

When the new government was organized, President Washington appointed John Jay to be the first Chief Justice of the Supreme Court. The position carries more prestige now than in the nation's earliest years. While serving on the bench, Jay ran unsuccessfully for elected office and accepted a diplomatic mission to Great Britain. Finally, he resigned from the fledgling court in 1796 to take a more important job, as Governor of New York.

regions and would provide strong leadership for a people who had become weary from the sacrifices of war and indifferent to public matters. Let us begin by considering what representation meant on the eve of the Constitutional Convention.

Virtue

A revolution in political behavior accompanied America's revolt against British rule. The transformation had begun earlier in a few, especially heterogeneous colonies such as New York and Pennsylvania. There, as early as the 1730s, the competition among religious sects and commercial interests for control of the colonial assembly and the governor's office had changed the tempo and ethics of political life. After 1764, the hated British stamp taxes incited defiance of the law and an explosion of political activity in every colony. The politics of deference gave way to electioneering, party slates, and open challenges to the wisdom and loyalty of long-esteemed leaders. The meaning of representation had begun to change.

Beginning in 1776, patriots assembled to draft state constitutions. Every one of the new constitutions contained statements of principle and practical provisions to ensure that elected lawmakers faithfully carried out their constituents' desires. They called for open viewing galleries in the legislature, published reports of the legislative sessions, and instructions binding on the representatives. All were intended to make legislators fully accountable to the electorate. The state legislature served less as a gathering of wise men in search of right answers than as a forum for conflicting economic interests, ethnic groups, and religious sects. The representative was an agent, a servant of the people, expected to speak for and be like his constituents. After 1776, the ideal of a community governed by sage old leaders and bound together by shared values and common interests seemed nostalgic. Deferential politics slowly yielded to contentious, interest group politics.[217]

To invent a plan of national government suited to these new American political manners became the task of the Federal Convention in 1787. The Convention delegates admonished one another again and again to create not an ideal government but one the people would actually adopt. Yet comparing the United States Constitution with the earlier state constitutions can be misleading. Such a comparison is no measure of the Constitution's fidelity to the principles of the American Revolution. The choice confronting the Convention was not as simple as the triumph or rejection of the new popular politics. The complexity arose from the founders' belief in a common national interest, a concept that most Antifederalists steadfastly denied, and their determination to design a national legislature capable of serving the common good.

Even in the twentieth century, the national constitutions of several western European nations have provided that popularly elected legislators represent the entire nation, not just their own constituents, and cannot be bound by instructions from their local electorates.[218] Implicit in these modern provisions is the conviction that what is in the national interest is not necessarily a mathematical average of all the separate, parochial interests represented.[219] The common good may not be readily identified with one set of policies as opposed to another set. Governing in the national interest means the attitude one brings to the task rather than the policies one supports. That commitment to the national interest has made the tension between the representative as an independent statesman and as an agent for his constituents an enduring one, not simply a temporary stage in the transition from premodern to democratic politics. It is a tension inherent in representative government.[220]

Although no similarly explicit provision can be found in the United States Constitution, the ideal of the independent statesman governing in the national interest is evident in our political culture. In 1835, Alexis de Tocqueville lamented that the Americans' "passion for equality" made them reject the most capable, learned men and favor politicians more like themselves. The same leveling impulse meant that the people made their representatives servile spokesmen for public opinion and denied them the independence to govern well. Tocqueville feared the demise of the leadership principle on which the Constitution had been constructed. But Tocqueville's observation has proved only half true. The ideal of leadership for the common good persists despite the democratic character of our politics. Political scientists have demonstrated that especially on certain types of issues, such as foreign affairs, members of Congress sometimes choose not to cater to their own constituents. The media recognize that the proper role of a representative is a question of enduring interest. As the 1984 presidential and congressional elections neared, the editors of *The New York Times* chose to reprint a two-hundred-year-old message they knew would be meaningful to modern readers, Edmund Burke's 1774 Address to the Electors of Bristol, England. In it Burke had declared

that a national legislature was "not a congress of ambassadors from different and hostile interests" with each member "serving as an agent or advocate against other agents and advocates." It was "a deliberative assembly of one nation, with one interest, that of the whole."[221]

The concept of a shared national interest inspired the framers as they considered the proper role of the representative. For the framers, the most awesome task of the Revolution had been to convince the inhabitants of thirteen separate colonies that there was a common interest to unite them in war and afterward. This conviction of a common interest underlay the ideal of representation—let us call it virtuous representation—that defined the purpose of the Senate. This same ideal also influenced somewhat the design of the House of Representatives, compromising its immediate responsiveness to local popular feelings. Lawmakers were to deliberate together to discover the national interest, resisting the temptation of personal gain and the selfish interests and passionate demands of their constituents. Believing in virtuous representation did not make the founders antidemocrats and counter-Revolutionaries. Nor were they antimodern thinkers yearning nostalgically for a simple, homogeneous republic free of interest group politics. Their speeches and writings were filled with commentaries on the contentious, divisive politics of a heterogeneous society and how best to mitigate its worst effects. They could believe in virtuous representation as the central principle of leadership because they were confident that they would supply the corps of virtuous, enlightened leaders committed to governing in the national interest.

The framers went to the Constitutional Convention to remedy the existing Confederation's lack of authority to legislate in matters of finance, commerce, and foreign policy. But many of them were also determined to solve another problem—the arbitrary, unjust, excessive laws enacted by the new state legislatures. In several states, it seemed, local majorities were turning government to their own advantage, ignoring the public good and the rights of minorities.[222] One remedy to faction that Madison posed at the Constitutional Convention and again in the famous essays by Publius during the ratification contest has received lavish attention from historians and political scientists. In *The Federalist* No. 10, Madison offered the simple maxim that by creating a large republic, "you take in a greater variety of parties and interests [and] . . . make it less probable that a majority of the whole will have a common motive to invade the rights of other citizens." In Madison's large republic theory, representing meant being like and speaking for one's own constituents. Interests were antagonistic, not shared or complementary. The theory was essentially negative—in the Congress, clashing factions would cancel one another and produce only a deadlock.[223]

Too little attention has been paid to the positive side of Madison's expectations. Independent, virtuous statesmen would also serve in Congress, producing wise and just laws in the national interest. The country, though troubled by differences between rich and poor, debtor and creditor, farmer and merchant, North and South, also shared common interests. Representation, even in the lower house, was not intended to simulate a gathering of all the people. Nor was the end result to be a stalemate in the legislature, as Madison's critics, such as Robert Dahl, have argued. The goal of Madison's plan of government was to pro-

tect individual rights but also to maximize good government. A government of inaction, lacking an effective majority, was not what the ardent nationalist Madison wanted. The purpose of representation, explained Publius in *The Federalist* No. 10, was "to refine and enlarge the public views" by passing them through a "chosen body of citizens" wise and patriotic enough not to sacrifice the common good to personal or partial considerations. Representation was the cure for a factious political culture.[224]

Madison understood that most citizens were disinclined to serve the common welfare. They busied themselves getting and spending and thought about government only when their private interests were at stake or their rights were imperiled. Such private citizens were called to public service or sacrifice only during rare times of crisis such as war. But the body politic was composed of two other elements as well: a small corps of virtuous statesmen who were devoted to governing as a lifelong calling; and the loathsome factious demagogues who, Madison feared, might occasionally wrest government from the hands of enlightened statesmen and use it for personal gain.

Throughout the revolutionary crisis, Americans had told themselves again and again that their fate hinged not on mere strength of arms but on their virtue. By virtue, they meant not merely personal goodness but also a readiness to serve the public good above private fortune. Virtue meant spartan self-sacrifice for the republic. By 1787, Americans had tired of the great effort for nationhood and had turned inward in search of private happiness. In the political rhetoric of the Confederation period, calls for public service went unanswered and were uttered with growing infrequency and hopelessness.

The science of politics dwelt increasingly on whether republican government was possible where public virtue was in short supply.[225] The task Madison undertook was to design a system of government in which leadership by a virtuous few would, in ordinary times, be sufficient to produce good government. Madison expected that the voters would choose their representatives from this corps of public-minded, career statesmen. In the event the voters disappointed these expectations, constitutional safeguards were in place to check the abuse of power.

Today social critics want government to promote a just society—not just an open, procedurally fair political process but an end product that is just. And increasingly, they look to professionals in the government bureaucracy—lawyers, social workers, scientists—and to the courts to produce what the democratic political process will not mandate. However, the majority of Americans still place their confidence in representative government rather than the bureaucracy and the judiciary. Few citizens would say that they vote for the *virtuous* candidate for Congress. The word sounds naive and ridiculous. But in fact, this is what we hope we are doing. In our time, most national problems seem to require too much knowledge of science, geography, or economics and too much commitment in terms of time and moral energy for the private citizen to devote. We elect our representatives and entrust government to them. We do not instruct them or vigilantly keep track of how they vote on most issues. For this reason, the Madisonian distinction between the private citizen and the public leader may be more important to Americans now than to preceding generations.

The House of Representatives

When the Constitutional Convention began its meetings in May 1787 the first task undertaken was to erect a national legislature and invest it with broad lawmaking powers. Most of the delegates agreed that the House of Representatives had to be close enough to the people to legitimately claim that the people's representatives made the law. Yet the purpose of the House was not to duplicate with mathematical exactness all the social and economic components of the society and to reflect every pulse and passion in public opinion. The House was intended to make decisions more favorable to the public good than if "the people themselves [had] convened for that purpose."[226] The goal of Madison and like-minded delegates was to balance republican values with independent statesmanship in the national interest.

The Virginia Plan, laid before the Convention on May 29, called for direct popular election of the lower house.[227] The New England delegates Elbridge Gerry and Roger Sherman, still shaken from Shays' Rebellion and the popular demands for paper money and debtor relief legislation, spoke out against a House elected directly by the people. Liberty was as easily endangered by an excess of democracy as by too little, Sherman and Gerry warned. Let the state legislatures appoint sober, wise men to the national legislature.[228] But James Wilson and other supporters of the Virginia Plan countered that the people were the legitimate source of all governing authority. To claim legitimacy and win the confidence of the people the new government had to rest on a broad base, a popularly chosen lower house. A majority at the Convention agreed.[229]

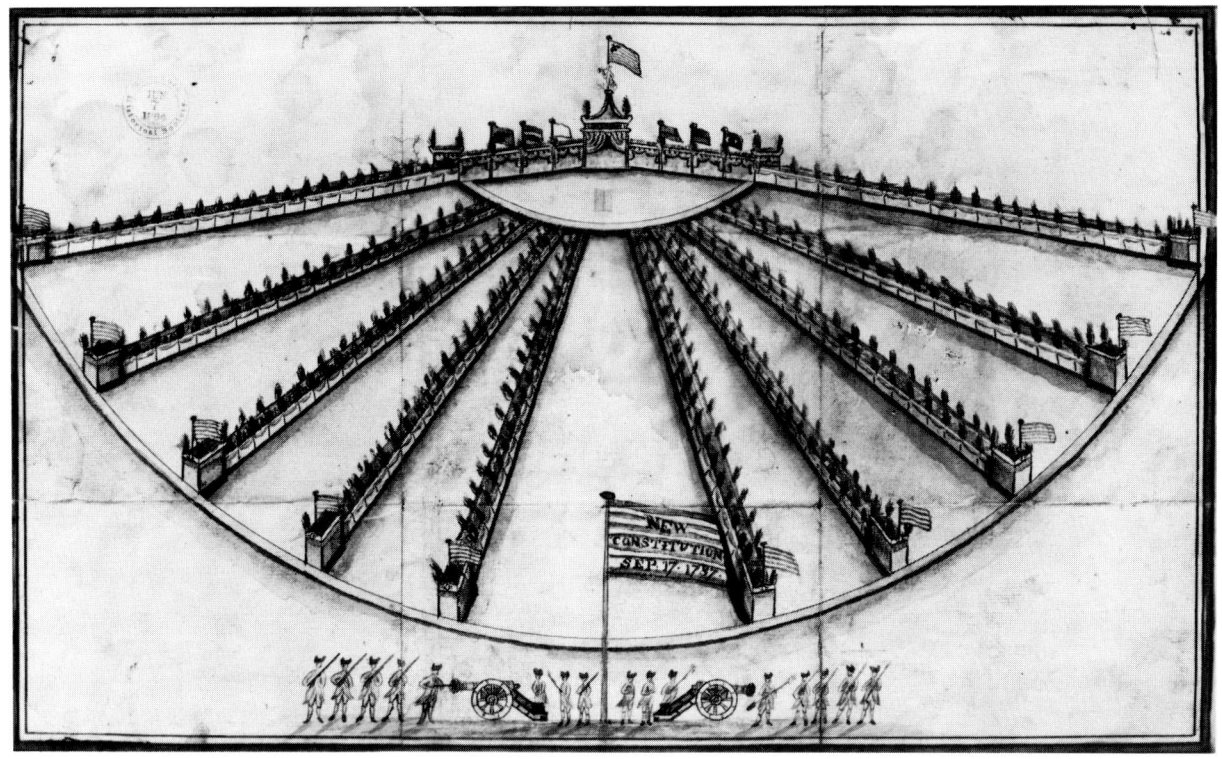

David Grim. *Banquet Pavilion*, undated. Watercolor on paper. Gift of Sophia Minton. 1864.17.

New York City gave a huge party on July 23, 1788, celebrating the nation's new Constitution. This watercolor depicts the Banquet Pavilion erected for the celebration. The pavilion was designed by Major Pierre Charles L'Enfant and was erected where Broadway and Broome Street now intersect. Ten tables were arranged in a rising sun pattern to represent the ten states that had already ratified the United States Constitution and to accommodate the five thousand marchers who turned out that day.

The people were empowered to elect their representatives directly, frequently, and proportionally, but even the members of the lower house were not to be mere agents for their constituents. At the Constitutional Convention, John Rutledge proposed that any candidate for the House of Representatives be required to have resided in the state for at least seven years prior to his election from that state. But the determined nationalist George Read retorted that "such a regulation would correspond little with the idea that we were one people." The majority agreed and rejected Rutledge's motion.[230]

One way to ensure that eminent, wise, virtuous representatives be chosen was to make the election districts large, explained Publius in *The Federalist* No. 10.[231] No other aspect of the new Constitution excited more criticism during the ratification struggle. Many of the issues pitting Antifederalists against the friends of the Constitution were regional or local, but the controversy over the size of the House of Representatives occurred everywhere. In every state ratifying convention, the Antifederalists complained that the House was too small "to make representation real and actual," a "true picture of the people." Sixty-five members chosen from large election districts would not know the circumstances of every county and corner in the state. Even worse, these sixty-five would lack that sympathy and fellow feeling for the great body of the voters that only men of middling rank could feel. The people, Antifederalists feared, would always vote first for the few prominent figures in the district—men of wealth, education, political experience, and influence. A much larger House was needed, the Antifederalists insisted, to bring in representatives like the people themselves, from every occupation and location. "The knowledge necessary for the representatives of a free people," Melancton Smith told the New York convention, "not only comprehends the extensive political and commercial information, such as is acquired by men of refined education," but also the common understanding shared by men in like circumstances.[232]

In response to this persistent grievance, the Federalists did not deny that the House was too small to provide an accurate portrait of the people. Instead they dismissed the very notion that representation was to imitate life. Mimetic representation was neither possible nor desirable. "The actual representation of all classes of people by persons of each class" Alexander Hamilton called "altogether visionary." Artisans and small farmers were sensible that they lacked the "acquired endowment" to govern well. They would always prefer wealthy landowners, merchants, and learned professionals. And "can it be objectionable," James Wilson asked the Pennsylvania ratifying convention, "that men should be employed that are most noted for their virtue and talents?" Wilson, like many other Federalists, talked about a "natural aristocracy." Abilities, not property or hereditary distinctions, made men fit to govern. Yet these abilities were hardly natural. They were acquired and, in the eighteenth century, somewhat more class

related than they are today. Humble citizens, explained Hamilton, "were sensible that their habits in life" had not given them "these acquired endowments, without which in a deliberative assembly the greatest natural abilities" were "useless."[233]

The spirit of equality is so much a part of our twentieth-century way of thinking that we have very little understanding of, or sympathy for, the Federalists' notion of a natural aristocracy. It is easy to assume that if wealthy men occupied nearly all the offices of government, they must have maintained their authority through coercion, deception, or corrupt influence. But deference to distinguished leaders who possessed the acquired capabilities to govern well was a voluntary act and not an entirely passive one. Wealth alone did not make anyone fit to govern, and voters knew that their task was to choose the men of true virtue and reject the counterfeit ones.[234] In the 1790s, the many ambitious proposals for higher education, which insisted that the public virtue of the nation's future leaders had to be cultivated in the classroom, remind us that sheer riches were not enough to make a good public leader.

It is often argued that the framers were antidemocrats who employed the rhetoric of the revolution ingenuously to thwart its principles. In these interpretations, the Constitution legitimated an aristocratic regime for the protection of property and privilege.[235] Like Charles Beard's *Economic Interpretation of the Constitution*, these newer and more sophisticated class interpretations reflect our failure to disregard how we think politics works today, that is, to put aside whatever cynicism we bring to contemporary political rhetoric in order to understand the eighteenth century on its own terms. A careful reading of early republican literature suggests that for the Federalists the most important issue was not class politics. It was how to erect a constitution that guaranteed self-government but also promoted good government by attracting the most able, virtuous men to public service and affording them the latitude to lead. How did the Federalists answer their adversaries' repeated complaints that the new government was aristocratic? A few Federalists denied that there was any conflict of interest between classes. The mechanic and the merchant both stood to benefit from commercial prosperity under a strong, solvent government. Small and great farmers alike shared a common fate in agriculture. Hamilton, for one, insisted on this commonality of interests. But many more Federalists were painfully aware of class antagonism. "Those who hold and those who are without property have ever formed distinct interests in society," wrote Madison. He called the inequality of wealth "the most common and durable source of faction."[236] The most important and frequent Federalist answer to Antifederalist cries of aristocracy was that there were men from privileged backgrounds who had an honest desire to serve the common welfare and who would not automatically equate the immediate interests of their own class with the common good.

Whether it was possible for any public servant to look beyond his own self-interest and govern with disinterested justice was precisely the question Madison posed in *The Federalist* No. 10: "No man is allowed to be a judge in his own cause, because his interest would certainly bias his judgement, and, not improbably, corrupt his integrity," Madison began. "Yet what are many of the most important acts of legisla-

tion but so many judicial determinations . . . concerning the rights of large bodies of citizens? And what are the different classes of legislators but advocates and parties to the causes which they determine?" Madison supplied the answer himself, announcing that the purpose of representation in the new plan was to entrust government to a chosen body of public servants who were wise enough to understand the true interests of their country and patriotic enough to ignore all other considerations.[237]

Again in *The Federalist* No. 57, Madison squarely addressed the enormous controversy over the size of the House of Representatives. The objective, he announced, was not to achieve the most immediate and accurate representation of the people but rather "to obtain for rulers men who possess the most wisdom to discern, and the most virtue to pursue, the common good of society."[238] Federalist pamphleteer Noah Webster told his readers that "the design of representation [was] to bring the collective interest into view." When the Antifederalist Melancton Smith warned the New York ratifying convention that a small House of Representatives could not know and guard the particular interests of every part of the state, Alexander Hamilton snapped back that such interests had already "too often been preferred to the welfare of the Union." And James Wilson lectured Pennsylvania Antifederalists that a congressman's duty was to govern for the whole nation, not merely for his own neighborhood. The larger the congressional district, the more likely that talented, virtuous men would be elected, and "the more agreeable it [was] to the constitutional principle of representation."[239]

The Antifederalists were also troubled that the two-year term would make members of the House independent and remote from the voters. At the Convention, Madison had supported a three-year term to enable the representatives to acquire an understanding of the needs and interests of the other states. But Gerry of Massachusetts had admonished the delegates that the people of New England would never tolerate any departure from annual elections. Every state except South Carolina had provided in its state constitution for yearly elections of its lower house.[240] The delegates had compromised on two years, but Gerry's forebodings soon proved to be accurate. At the Massachusetts ratifying convention, Federalists were challenged again and again to defend biennial elections. In response, the Massachusetts Federalist Fisher Ames urged that representation was not simply a gathering of public opinion but "something more than the people." It required prudent reflection and a knowledge of the other states.[241]

The most important debate on the meaning of representation occurred in August 1789 as the House of Representatives prepared a Bill of Rights. One congressman proposed that the list include the people's right to issue instructions to their representatives. Antifederalist Aedanus Burke argued for the proposal, warning that the people would not settle for less. He pointed to provisions for instructions in several state constitutions. Other Antifederalists had demanded a provision for binding instructions during the ratifying debates. Moderate Federalists in Congress understood how urgent it was to produce a Bill of Rights in order to quiet the remaining public doubts and divisions over the new Constitution. But they rejected the demand for binding instructions because the overriding purpose of the national legislature was "to consult for the common good." The proposal was defeated ten to forty-one. Binding instructions, Federalist George Clymer explained, would have made Congress "a mere passive machine" reacting to popular opinion rather than an independent, deliberative body. "Can it be supposed that the inhabitants of a single district in a State," asked Thomas Hartley, "are better informed with respect to the general interests of the Union than a select body assembled from every part?"[242] The fatal flaw of the old Congress, remembered Madison, was that its members acted as partisans of local interests instead of "impartial guardians of a common interest."[243]

The Senate

Despite the constitution makers' commitment to the national interest, creating a lower house to advance that interest was problematic. They were acutely aware of the people's new political expectations and the necessity to meet them. The people demanded direct, frequent, popular elections. Inevitably, the representative's freedom to apply his expertise and wider vision to the task of governing would be small. But when the framers designed the Senate, they made representation an act of reason and deliberation.

From the outset, the framers never doubted that there would be an upper house. They reasoned that dividing the lawmaking power between two houses would prevent unfaithful legislators from betraying the people's trust.[244] But the Senate was to achieve more than a Whiggish check on the abuse of power. It was also to provide an antidote to the "turbulence and follies" of a lower house that carried out the people's will too faithfully.[245] Publius explained that the Senate's longer term, in-

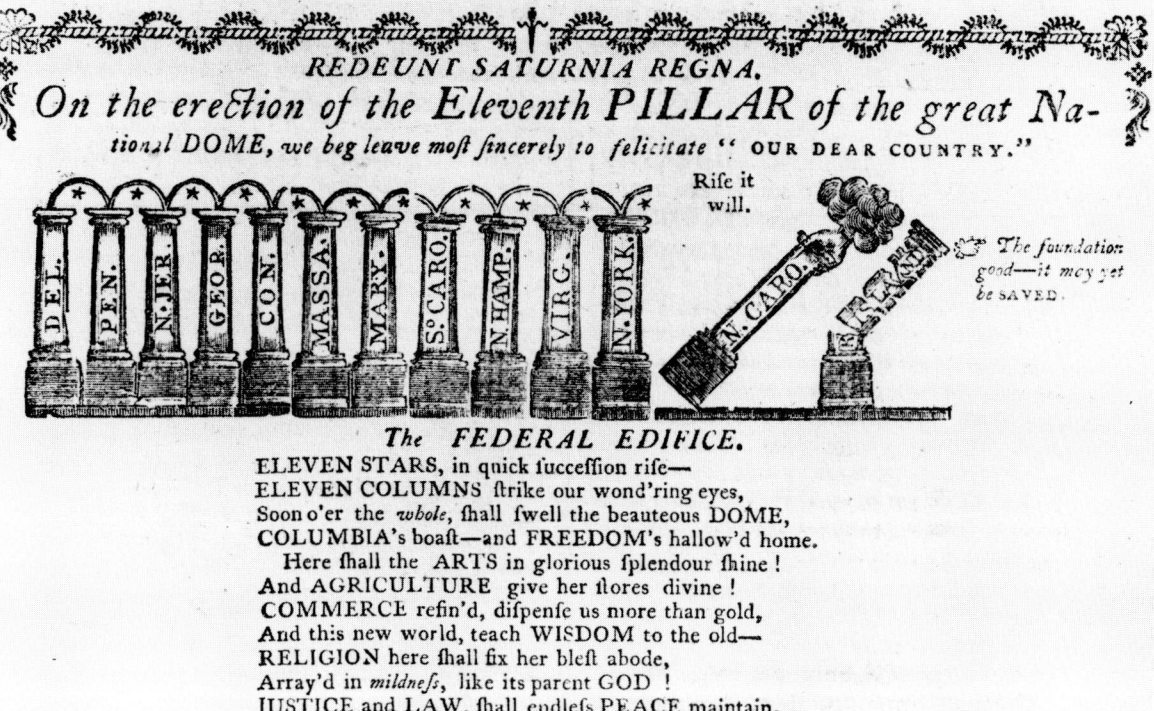

REDEUNT SATURNIA REGNA.

On the erection of the Eleventh PILLAR of the great National DOME, we beg leave most sincerely to felicitate " OUR DEAR COUNTRY."

Rise it will.

☞ The foundation good—it may yet be SAVED.

The FEDERAL EDIFICE.

ELEVEN STARS, in quick succession rise—
ELEVEN COLUMNS strike our wond'ring eyes,
Soon o'er the *whole*, shall swell the beauteous DOME,
COLUMBIA's boast—and FREEDOM's hallow'd home.
Here shall the ARTS in glorious splendour shine !
And AGRICULTURE give her stores divine !
COMMERCE refin'd, dispense us more than gold,
And this new world, teach WISDOM to the old—
RELIGION here shall fix her blest abode,
Array'd in *mildness*, like its parent GOD !
JUSTICE and LAW, shall endless PEACE maintain,
And *the* " SATURNIAN AGE," *return again.*

Cartoon from the *Massachusetts Centinel*, August 2, 1788.

When news reached Massachusetts that the Poughkeepsie convention had ratified the Constitution, the *Centinel* published this cartoon, celebrating New York as the eleventh pillar of the great national edifice. Similar images, depicting the ratifying states as sturdy neoclassical columns, appeared frequently in newspapers everywhere.

direct election, and small size made it as different from the House as possible without abandoning popular representation altogether.[246]

The Senate was envisioned as a small, deliberating body "respectable for its wisdom and virtue" and free of the "passionate proceedings" that commonly troubled larger assemblies.[247] A lengthy term was to make it firm, independent, and stable enough to resist the swings in popular opinion felt in the lower house. Despite reminders from Roger Sherman and Elbridge Gerry that the people would expect fre-

quent, even annual, elections, the Convention decided that senators would serve for six years.[248] The lengthy term had another purpose as well: to make the senatorial office attractive to career statesmen. The Senate's task, argued Publius, required persons committed to governing as a lifelong calling, who devoted their time to studying the laws and interests of the country. Madison disparaged the ideal of the private person—the Cincinnatus—who was drafted to serve the public but returned to the plow at the first opportunity. Cincinnatus was an appropriate hero for the Antifederalists, who distrusted government. Madison warned that persons called "from pursuits of a private nature [and] continued in appointment for a short time" lacked the expertise to govern well.[249] In contrast, Antifederalists objected that the six-year term would allow senators to grow independent and forgetful of the people.[250]

The framers' first accomplishment was in determining what the Senate could never be. Would the upper house be an American House of Lords to speak for the nation's wealthy? Or a confederate body to represent the state governments, as under the old Congress? In the process of making practical decisions about the term, powers, and method of choosing the upper house, the framers examined and discarded these old, inappropriate models, clearing the way for a new American rationale for bicameralism.

Because the Convention allowed every state two seats in the Senate and empowered the state legislatures to choose the senators, many Americans at the time and ever since have incorrectly assumed that the framers intended senators to represent the state governments. What made the confusion worse is that Madison occasionally encouraged that belief. He understated the Convention's radical departure from Confederation government to increase the chances for ratification. In *The Federalist* No. 39, he even called the Senate the "federal" house.[251] What actually happened at the Constitutional Convention shows how few of the framers, and none less than Madison, conceived of the Senate in this way.

The Connecticut delegates insisted that state politicians would have to be wooed into supporting the new government. Allowing them to choose the Senate was one way to do it. The Convention saw the wisdom of this and agreed that the members of the Senate would be chosen by the state legislatures.[252] Madison demanded a system of proportional representation because he wanted each citizen, not each state, to have an equal voice in the legislature. On this question, most of the other delegates voted not for a theory but for practical results. The extreme nationalist George Read, who had firmly opposed allowing the state legislatures to choose senators, insisted on equal representation for every state because the people of Delaware would not accept less. Massachusetts's Elbridge Gerry and South Carolina's Charles Pinckney had earnestly supported election of the Senate by the state legislatures. But they opposed an equality of votes in the Senate because it would not benefit the large and Southern states.[253] Neither the state legislatures' role in selecting the Senate nor the equality of representation there meant a retreat from national government to a confederate one. Explaining the equality of the states in the upper house, Publius confessed, "It is superfluous to try, by the standard of theory, a part of the constitution which is allowed on all hands to be the result not of theory," but a practical compromise between the large and small states.[254] As to the role of senators, though chosen by the state legislatures, they were not mere agents for them. As soon as the contest between small and large states was settled, the Convention agreed that each senator would cast his vote individually, not as part of a state delegation. Luther Martin opposed the decision, arguing that the Senate was supposed to represent the states. But a large majority of the delegates would not sacrifice public virtue to state interests. Even Oliver Ellsworth of Connecticut, one of the delegates who had fought tirelessly for equal representation in the

Charles Willson Peale. *Samuel Blachley Webb*, 1779. Miniature on ivory. Gift of Colonel G. Creighton Webb. 1939.50.

On July 27, 1788, Samuel B. Webb, a handsome, thirty-five year old brigadier general stationed in New York, wrote to his fiancée at Boston, "The Mail brought us the pleasing intelligence of our Convention at Poughkeepsie haveing agreed to adopt the New Constitution.—It was received with unusual marks of Joy; every class of Citizens turned out, Bells rang—Cannon fired, fireworks were displayed . . . and continued untill past 8 o'clock this morning—indeed I am afraid that Sunday would not bring them to their usual steadiness." The following April, Webb paraded as the grand marshall at George Washington's inauguration.

In the spring of 1789, Webb sent this ivory miniature to his beloved, Catherine Hogeboom, adding that when it was painted in 1779, it had been an excellent likeness, but eleven years had made a "material change" in a soldier's face.

upper house, agreed that he had always envisioned senators voting individually.[255]

Twice the Convention considered whether congressmen would be paid by their state governments or by the nation. Madison argued that senators, at least, had to be paid out of the national treasury. Making the Senate dependent on the states would "subvert" its purpose as a "firm, wise, and impartial body." Senators at the mercy of the states for their livelihood would be "the mere Agents & Advocates of

State interests & views, instead of . . . impartial umpires & Guardians of justice and the General Good."[256] John Dickinson of Delaware said he presumed that all the delegates "were convinced of the necessity of making the Genl. Govt. independent of the prejudices, passions, and improper views of the State Legislatures." Congressmen had to be free to deliberate in the national interest without fear that their state governments would cut off their salaries. Luther Martin, who had no vision of a national interest binding the separate states, countered that the Senate was intended to represent the states and ought to be paid by the states. His fellow Maryland delegate Daniel Carroll shot back that "the Senate was to represent & manage the affairs of the whole nation," not the parochial concerns of the states. A majority of the delegates, from the small and large states alike, agreed with Carroll. Envisioning that congressmen should govern in the national interest, the Convention voted on August 14 to pay them out of the national treasury.[257]

The important disagreement over the proper role of the senator occurred between Federalists and Antifederalists after the Convention. The people who ratified the Constitution decided what it meant, and they repudiated the notion that a senator represented his state government. Consider the debate in the New York ratifying convention on an amendment proposed by Antifederalist George Livingston entitling the state legislature to recall errant senators. Livingston feared a Senate grown remote, permanent, and independent.[258] Antifederalists John Lansing and Melancton Smith, insisting that senators were "agents" acting on behalf of the state governments, supported recall to ensure their "strict subordination."[259] But the Federalists countered successfully that recall

would defeat the senator's purpose. "It will destroy that spirit of independence and free deliberation. . . . Whenever the interests of a state clash with those of the Union, it will oblige him to sacrifice the great objects of his appointment to local attachments."[260]

Wisdom and impartiality, not wealth, were to be given a house of their own. Early state constitution makers had struggled to imitate the British model of mixed government. Though there was no legally distinct nobility to give substance to a House of Lords in America, some states had reserved the upper house exclusively for the rich. The framers rejected the mixed government model entirely. Both houses of Congress would represent all the people. James Wilson proudly explained to the Pennsylvania ratifying convention that distinct ways of representing the people replaced the separate estates of mixed government in the new Constitution.[261] Among all the framers, only Alexander Hamilton and Gouverneur Morris questioned whether this new theory of bicameralism could work. Voicing a concern that many Antifederalists would raise during the ratification debates, Morris told the Convention how worried he was that "abilities and virtue" were not enough to distinguish the upper house from the lower. "One interest [had to] be opposed to another interest" to make the upper house an effective check on the lower. The rich had to be pitted against the multitude controlling the popular branch.[262]

The often overlooked Convention debates on a money bill provision are especially revealing. On June 13, Elbridge Gerry asked the Convention to "restrain the Senatorial branch from originating money bills." The other branch was "more immediately the representatives of the people," he said, "and it was a maxim that the people ought to hold the purse strings." Most of the delegates rejected Gerry's reasoning. "We were always following the British Constitution when the reason of it did not apply," said Pierce Butler. "There was no analogy between the House of Lords" and the Senate. Madison insisted that "the Senate would be the representatives of the people as well as the 1st branch." Roger Sherman added that senatorial wisdom was "particularly needed in the finance business." The delegates defeated Gerry's motion three to eight.[263]

What was rejected in principle on June 13 and again on June 26 was later employed as a concession to the large states to resolve the dangerously divisive controversy over the ratio of representation in the legislature. The committee that reported a compromise plan on July 5 recommended that "bills for raising or appropriating money" had to originate in the lower house, where proportional representation gave the large states a majority. Benjamin Franklin, who probably suggested the concession, urged its adoption. The most stalwart large state delegates were still determined to thwart any compromise, and they insisted that the concession was not enough to mitigate the injustice of allowing each state an equal vote in the upper house. These delegates reminded the Convention that the money bill provision was inconsistent with the new American understanding of what an upper house was for. "It would make it a constitution principle that the 2d branch was not possessed of the confidence of the people," objected one Massachusetts delegate. But the spokesmen for compromise prevailed. The money bill provision was adopted on July 6. The following morning, the Convention agreed to give each state equal representation in the upper house.[264]

Despite its usefulness as a point of compromise, the money bill provision made most of the delegates uneasy. Charles Pinckney had little trouble persuading the Convention to strike it out on August 8. Only the persistent warnings of Edmund Randolph, George Mason, Benjamin Franklin, and Oliver Ellsworth—architects and defenders of the compromise on representation—finally persuaded most of the delegates to reinstate the money bill provision on September 8 before the entire compromise came unhinged.[265]

Throughout the ratification ordeal, Antifederalists emphatically denied that an upper house of wisdom, talent, and devotion to the common good could be relied on to check the popular lower house. Such a Senate was a mere artificial creation, insisted Richard Henry Lee, who wrote as the "Federal Farmer." It lacked the weighty authority and separate interests of an aristocratic branch. And it presumed a naive view of human nature.[266] "Tell me not of checks on paper, but tell me of checks founded on self love," demanded Patrick Henry.[267] The constitution makers were repeatedly assailed for their foolhardy vision of a corps of virtuous leaders. "Disinterested patriotism," Henry warned, had never been relied on by "an enlightened, free people. If you depend on your Presidents' and senators' patriotism, you are gone."[268] It was the Antifederalists, not the architects of the Constitution, who doubted that a government by the people, unchecked by a rival, aristocratic branch, could work.

Just how good or evil men were became the question dividing the Virginia ratifying convention. Henry issued lengthy diatribes on the "depraved nature of man." In rebuttal, Edmund Randolph urged his fellow Virginians to be reasonable. He reminded them that vigilance and a cautious distrust of those who govern could be carried to such lengths that it was "degrading and humiliating to human nature." Randolph called it inconceivable that representatives "selected for [their] superior qualities" would "suddenly be changed from upright men to monsters" when they took office.[269]

Yet the new plan of government was hardly constructed on a roseate vision of human nature. The selfish impulses that gave rise to factions could not be eliminated, Publius told the readers of *The Federalist* No. 10. In devising a representative legislature for a modern, pluralistic society, interest had to be countered by competing interest. To ensure that no department of government exceeded its powers, institutional checks and balances were constructed, "supplying by opposite and rival interests, the defect of better motives."[270] But what distinguished the Federalists from their opponents was their vision of a shared national interest and a corps of national leaders. While most men were absorbed in private pursuits, giving little thought to public matters unless their own interests were at stake, a corps of enlightened, career statesmen would serve the common good. Some faith was necessary that those chosen for their virtue and wisdom would not betray the public trust. Institutional checks and balanced interests alone could never guarantee good government. "The power of doing good is inseparable from that of doing some evil," John Marshall admitted to the Virginia ratifying convention.[271]

A Union Consecrated in Blood

The ideal of virtuous, independent leadership in the national interest guided the founders as they invented the Senate and the House of Representatives. Historians eyeing the economic, religious, and geographic tensions troubling the new nation and the contentious political style that these provoked have dismissed this ideal as "utopian" and "divorced from the realities of American society." The future of American political thought, it has been argued, "lay with the doctrine of actual representation."[272] But the ideal of independent statesmanship for the common good comported well with another aspect of the founders' environment, the recent and vividly remembered Continental war effort. Madison's essay on American pluralism and political factionalism, *The Federalist* No. 10, is the most thoroughly analyzed piece of political writing by any of the founders. *The Federalist* No. 41 is rarely mentioned. In it, Madison appealed to Americans not to forget the shared national interest that transcended their differences. Disregard, he urged, the woeful Antifederalist message that a diverse, sometimes divided nation cannot live under one government. "Hearken not to the unnatural voice which tells you that the people of America . . . can no longer live together as members of the same family . . . the kindred blood which flows in the veins of American citizens, the mingled blood which they have shed in defence of their sacred rights, consecrate their Union."[273]

Items Exhibited

I. In Quest of Union

1. Declaration of Independence, 1st printing. Philadelphia, printed by John Dunlap, 1776.

The sovereignty of the people, the Declaration of Independence stated, was self-evident. The people had the right to institute their own government and define its powers.

2. Thirteen-star United States flag. Hand-woven cotton. 1939.559. See illustration, page 25.

3. *Articles of Confederation and Perpetual Union.* . . . Lancaster, printed by Francis Bailey, 1777. Signed by Henry Laurens, President of Congress.

America's first constitution was the Articles of Confederation, drafted in 1776 and 1777 by the members of the Continental Congress and finally ratified by the thirteen states in 1781.

4. "Map of the British and French Dominions in North America. . . ." Drawn by John Mitchell in 1755. (Third edition, London, 1755). Gift of Peter Jay. See illustration, page 15.

5. Giuseppe Ceracchi. *John Jay*, 1792. Plaster bust. X.52. See illustration, page 98.

6. John Adams, letter to Rufus King, June 14, 1786.

John Adams, envoy to Great Britain, wrote despairingly to Rufus King that the new American nation was humiliated abroad. The individual states refused to honor the terms of the Treaty of Paris, and the weak Confederation government was powerless to compel their compliance. "If the Faith of the Nation cannot be depended on, . . . it will never be respected or confided in at home or abroad."

7. Benjamin Lincoln, letter to Rufus King, February 11, 1786.

Benjamin Lincoln, a Massachusetts farmer and continental statesman, warned King that merely enlarging the lawmaking powers of Congress would not remedy the grave problems facing the nation. A central government empowered to enforce, rather than merely recommend, was needed.

8. Rufus King, letter to Elbridge Gerry, March 29, 1786.

Rufus King, a Massachusetts lawyer and

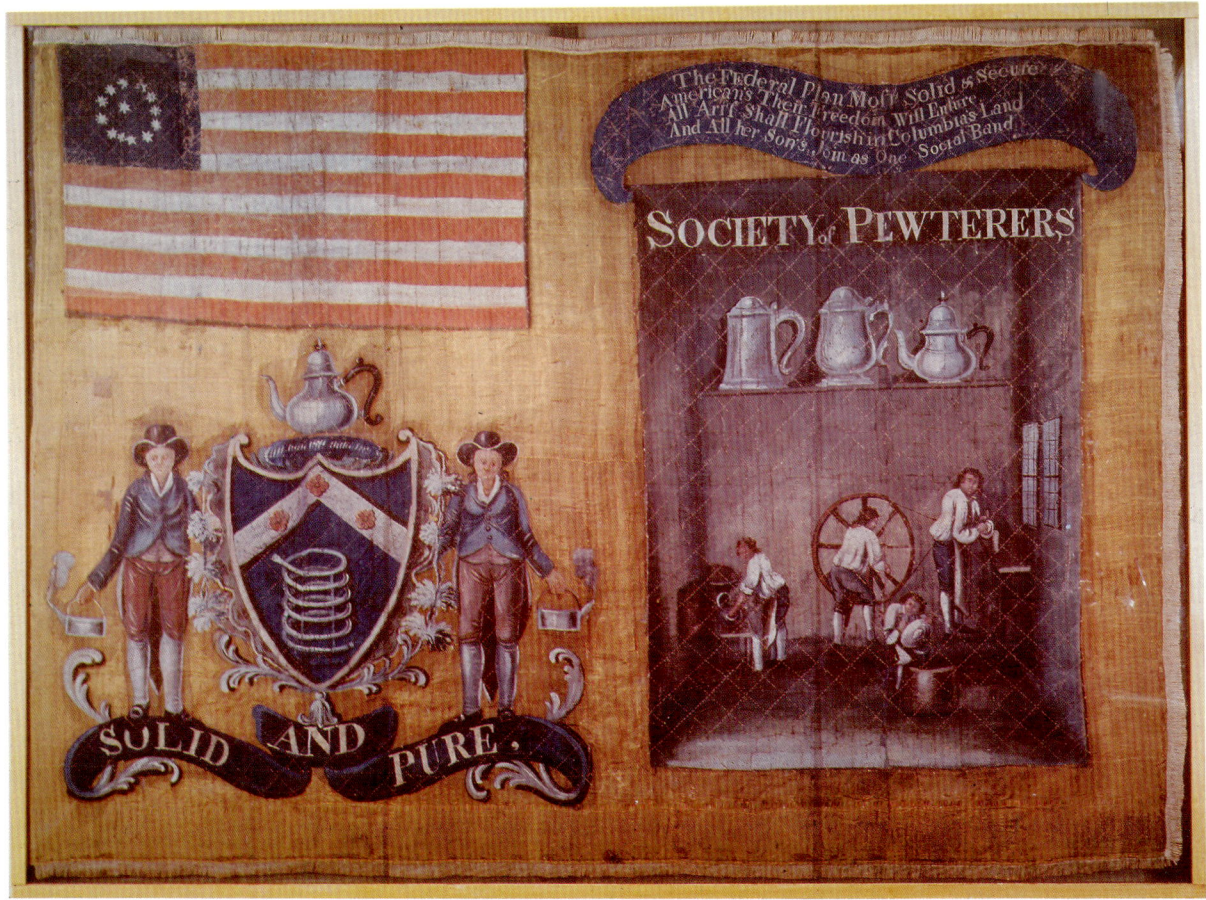

Painted silk banner carried in the Federal Procession at New York City, July 23, 1788. Gift of Mr. James S. Haring, 1903.12; restored by Ms. Kathryn Scott, 1974.

On July 23, 1788, New York City celebrated the adoption of the United States Constitution with cannon fire, bell ringing, and a grand parade and outdoor banquet. More than five thousand people marched in the Federal Procession. This painted silk banner was carried by the Society of Pewterers, one of the many working men's associations that marched. Pictured on the banner are a thirteen-star flag—although only ten states had ratified—a coat of arms inscribed "Solid and Pure," and the interior of a pewterer's shop. The New York State convention, already meeting at Poughkeepsie, ratified the Constitution three days later.

man of public affairs, served in the old Congress under the Articles of Confederation.

In the spring of 1786, King reported that once again Congress had requested but failed to secure the authority to tax trade. The consent of all thirteen states was required to augment the powers of Congress. This time New York had withheld its approval. The New York Assembly was to consider the issue again, but the outcome was "extremely doubtful."

9. Rufus King, letter to John Adams, May 5, 1786.

"That there exists a criminal neglect of

several of the states in their most important duties to the confederacy cannot be denied. I hope a reform will take place."

10. *The New-York City Directory.* New York, printed by Shepard Kollock, 1786. Page 53.

Listed are the president and other members of Congress, which met in New York City under the authority of the Articles of Confederation.

11. Rembrandt Peale. *Thomas Jefferson*, 1805. Oil on canvas. Gift of Thomas J. Bryan, 1867.306. See illustration, page 19.

12. *Providence Gazette and Country Journal*, February 10, 1787. Page 1.

From September 1786 to February 1787, debt-ridden farmers in Massachusetts resorted to mob action. They were angered by the scarcity of hard currency to pay their taxes and mortgages and the refusal of the state government to print paper money. Fearing foreclosures against their farms and imprisonment for debt, they used violence to force the courts to close. The rioters even attacked the federal arsenal at Springfield. Shays' Rebellion, named for its leader Daniel Shays, was reported widely in the press.

13. *Maryland Journal and Baltimore Advertiser*, February 20, 1787. Page 3.

Newspapers everywhere contained long, lurid accounts of Shays' Rebellion.

II. The Grand Convention at Philadelphia

14. Rembrandt Peale. *George Washington*, 1835. Oil on canvas. Bequest of Caroline Phelps Stokes, 1910.3. See illustration, page 12.

15. Asher B. Durand. *James Madison*, 1835. Oil on canvas. Gift of the New York Gallery of Fine Arts, 1858.10. See illustration, page 17.

16. Nathan Dane, letter to Rufus King, June 19, 1787.

From New York, Nathan Dane wrote that he fully agreed with the Convention's decision to keep its proceedings secret.

17. Henry Bryan Hall after Joseph Wood. *Rufus King*, ca. 1850–1884. Engraving.

Rufus King represented Massachusetts at the Constitutional Convention, where he lent unwavering support to James Madison's campaign for a strong, national system.

18. Rufus King. Convention notes. June 4, 6, 1787.

To thwart the making of unjust or imprudent laws, a check on the legislature was necessary. Madison doubted that a presidential veto would work. A single man occupying the executive office would not have the preeminence and popular support needed to resist the will of a majority of Congress. He proposed joining the justices of the Supreme Court with the president to form a council of revision, which would be "respectable" enough to veto decisions of Congress.

On June 4 and again on June 6, the Convention debated and rejected Madison's proposal. A majority of the delegates insisted that the judge's duty, as expositor of the laws, be kept separate from the lawmaker's role. King recorded in his notes: "There is a Difference—the Judges must interpret the Laws they ought not be legislators."

19. Rufus King. Convention notes. June 13, 1787.

On June 13, the Convention agreed to review the proposals agreed to so far. Despite the bitter dispute between small and large states, the delegates had approved nineteen resolutions, including "that a national government ought to be established."

20. Rufus King. Convention notes. June 16, 1787.

On June 16, the strident New York anti-nationalist John Lansing contrasted the Virginia Plan to the existing "federal" government under the Articles of Confederation. He admonished the Convention not to attempt a wholly new, untried form of government. Lansing had little faith that reason could achieve what history suggested was not possible: "Experience don't warnt our forming a Nat'l. Govt.—Where we have no experience there can be no reliance on Reason."

21. Rufus King. Convention notes. June 18 (19), 1787.

Rufus King carefully defined the terms "national" and "federal" to distinguish the Virginia Plan from the existing federal system. A government capable of enforcing its laws directly on individual citizens, with-

Giuseppe Ceracchi. *John Jay,* 1792. Plaster bust. X.52.

John Jay served the Confederation as Secretary of Foreign Affairs from 1784 to 1789. John Adams, Minister to Great Britain, received word from Jay in February 1787 that "our government is unequal to the task assigned it, and the people begin also to perceive its inefficiency. The Convention gains ground." Jay was here referring to support for the forthcoming gathering in Philadelphia.

out relying on the cooperation of the state governments, was "national," said King. Although dated June 18, his remarks were offered on the nineteenth.

22. Rufus King. Convention notes. June 9, 1787.

On June 9, New Jersey's William Paterson, impatient under the aggressive leadership of the Virginians, raised the issue of representation in Congress. The Virginia Plan provided that representation in each house of Congress would be allocated to the states according to the sizes of their populations. In the angriest speech heard since the opening day, Paterson raged that

New Jersey would never agree to the Virginia Plan. New Jersey had fewer than 150,000 inhabitants, less than half the population of Massachusetts, Pennsylvania, or Virginia.

23. Rufus King. Convention notes. June 27 (28), 1787.

James Madison tried, in vain, to calm the mounting fears of the less populous states that a system of proportional representation would reduce them to mere vassals of Massachusetts, Pennsylvania, and Virginia. "No circumstance of Religion, Habits, manners, mode of thinking, course of Business, manufactures, commerce, or natural productions" would make the three most populous states voting partners in Congress against the smaller states.

24. Rufus King. Convention notes. June 29, 1787.

On June 29, Oliver Ellsworth of Connecticut appealed to the Convention to compromise, by allocating representation according to population in the lower house of Congress and allowing each state an equal voice in the upper house. "If we don't agree in this measure, we have met in vain."

25. Rufus King. Convention notes. May 31, 1787.

The Virginia Plan proposed that the members of the lower house of Congress be elected directly by the people. Elbridge Gerry of Massachusetts, trembling with the memory of Shays' Rebellion, objected to popular election. But George Mason, James Madison, and James Wilson argued, with success, that a government empowered to act directly on the people had to be chosen by the people. A direct popular election would secure the "Confidence" and inspire the "affection" of the citizenry.

26. Rufus King. Convention notes. August 8, 1787.

Nathaniel Gorham reminded the delegates that the states were accustomed to deciding who was entitled to vote. A uniform property requirement would fall leniently on some states and harshly on others, where land was scarce and more divided. It was prudent to leave the question, who could vote, in the hands of the states. "We must regard the habits and prejudices of the people," said Gorham.

27. Rufus King. Convention notes. August 7, 1787.

On August 7, Gouverneur Morris pressed the Convention to limit voting rights to men having a freehold, that is, owning a certain amount of property. Morris warned that if the propertyless were given votes, they would sell them to the rich: "There can be no Aristocracy if the Freeholders are Electors—but there will be, when a great rich man shall bring his indigent dependents to vote in Elections—if you don't establish a qualification of property, you will have an Aristocracy."

28. Jean Antoine Houdon. *Benjamin Franklin*, 1778. Plaster bust. 1937.315. See illustration, page 101.

29. "We the people . . . ," William Livingston's copy of the Report of the Committee of Style, September 8, 1787. Philadelphia, printed by Dunlap and Claypoole. See illustration, p. 70.

30. Jean Antoine Houdon. *George Washington*. Plaster bust. Gift of Dr. David Hosack, 1832.4.

Washington addressed the Convention only once. Jean Antoine Houdon was one of France's greatest sculptors in the eighteenth century. Houdon journeyed to the United States in 1785 and visited Mount Vernon, where he made a life mask of Washington. Later, Houdon modeled this bust in his Paris studio, from the life mask.

31. Alexandre Roslin. *Benjamin Franklin*, ca. 1789–1790, after Joseph S. Duplessis. Oil on canvas. The Louis Dorr Fund, 1892.8. See illustration, page 30.

32. *The American Museum, or Repository of Ancient and Modern Fugitive Pieces . . .* , June 1787. Philadelphia, printed by Mathew Carey. Page 482.

As the controversy over the adequacies of the Confederation excited the public's attention, Mathew Carey founded *The American Museum* in January 1787. This monthly magazine was devoted to reprinting and disseminating important political writings. Subscribers included nearly every American notable, among them George Washington and Benjamin Franklin. The poetry for June 1787 included an ode to the framers, "called from each sister realm, the wise and 'great' who held in their hands 'Columbia's mighty sway.' "

33. *The Columbia Magazine or Monthly Miscellany . . .* , July 1787. Philadelphia, printed for T. Seddon, etc. Foldout and page 511.

As the public waited anxiously for news of the Convention's work, *The Columbia Magazine* presented a view of the Pennsylvania State House where the delegates were meeting. The event occurring there, the editor judged, was "more interesting in the history of the world than any of the celebrated fabrics of Greece or Rome."

III. The New Plan of Government Unveiled

34. *Pennsylvania Packet and Daily Advertiser*, September 19, 1787. Pages 2–3.

Philadelphia editors rushed to print the new Constitution in the newspapers. Historians have speculated that the first newspaper to print was the Philadelphia *Evening Chronicle*, which appeared twice weekly on Tuesdays and Saturdays. But not one copy of the *Evening Chronicle* for Tuesday, September 18, has ever been found. Five Philadelphia papers carried front page versions of the Constitution on Wednesday, September 19. Of these five, only the *Pennsylvania Packet and Daily Advertiser* version was free of error.

35. *The Daily Advertiser*, September 21, 1787.

New Yorkers read the United States Constitution first in the *Daily Advertiser* and the *New-York Packet.*

36. *Plan of the New Constitution for the United States of America . . . with a Preface by the Editor.* London, printed for J. Debrett, 1787. Page 1.

Europeans waited anxiously for news of the Convention's work, and publishers hurried to print the new Constitution. The editor of this early London version announced that "the rise of a new Empire in the World, constituted on principles of Government essentially different from the old" would be watched attentively by European politicians.

37. "The News-Mongers' Song for the Winter of 1788," *Massachusetts Centinel,* Boston, December 1, 1787. Page 4.

Public excitement and controversy over the proposed new plan of government was "good news" for "dealers in metre & prose!" The newspaper man who wrote this song reveled in the booming demand for commentary on the Constitution: "Much joy, brother printers! The day is our own, a time like the present sure never was known." "The News-Mongers' Song" first appeared in the *Albany Gazette*, but editors liked its message and reprinted it in fourteen other papers.

IV. The Federalist

38. John Trumbull. *Alexander Hamilton,* after 1840. Oil on canvas. Gift of Thomas J. Bryan, 1867.305. See illustration, page 34.

39. *The Independent Journal or the General Advertiser,* October 27, 1787. Page 2.

The first *Federalist* essay appeared in the New York *Independent Journal* on October 27, 1787. Alexander Hamilton began by alerting his countrymen that a task of great significance and opportunity awaited them: "To decide the important question, whether societies of men are really capable or not of establishing good government from reflection and choice, or whether they are forever destined to depend for their political constitutions on accident and force."

40. [Alexander Hamilton, John Jay, James Madison], *The Federalist: A Collection of Essays . . . ,* 2 vols. New York, printed by J. and A. M'Lean, 1788. Volume 1, title page.

Between October 1787 and April 1788, the three anonymous writers rushed to complete seventy-six essays for the New York newspapers. All were signed "Publius." In April and May, publishers John and Archibald M'Lean issued two volumes reprinting the essays and adding several new ones.

The essays won immediate acclaim, and speculation mounted as to the true identity of "Publius." Many rumors pointed to Alexander Hamilton, as the owner of the volume exhibited here noted on the title page. The three authors kept their partnership a secret, even from George Washington, until after New York had ratified in July.

41. [Alexander Hamilton, John Jay, James Madison], *The Federalist: A Collection of Essays . . . ,* 2 vols. New York, printed by J. and A. M'Lean, 1788. Volume 2, page 188.

Alexander Hamilton wrote at least fifty of the *Federalist* essays, including the important No. 62. There he addressed the frequent complaints by Antifederalists that a six-year term for senators was excessively long.

42. John Jay. Original manuscript for *The Federalist* No. 64.

This essay, in the handwriting of John Jay, was discovered in a box of Jay family papers at the New-York Historical Society in 1959. The whereabouts of three other *Federalist* essays are known. No. 5 is at Columbia University; Nos. 3 and 4 are in private collections. None of the original essays by Madison or Hamilton has survived.

43. Joseph Wright. *John Jay,* 1786. Oil on canvas. Gift of John Pintard, 1817.5. See illustration, page 80.

44. *The New York Times*, November 19, 1959. Pages 1, 47.

This front-page *New York Times* story relates the discovery of an extremely rare manuscript, John Jay's handwritten original for *The Federalist*, No. 64. The discovery settled a long dispute over who had composed the essay, John Jay or Alexander Hamilton.

45. *The American Magazine, containing a Miscellaneous Collection of Original and other Valuable Essays in Prose and Verse . . .* , March 1788. New York, printed by S. and J. Loudon. Page 260.

The monthly *American Magazine*, published in New York under the editorship of Noah Webster, praised *The Federalist*, declaring that "it would be difficult to find a treatise, which, in so small a compass, contains so much valuable political information, or in which the true principles of republican government are unfolded with such precision."

46. [Alexander Hamilton, John Jay, James Madison], *Le Federaliste . . .* , Paris, published by Buisson, 1792. Volume 2, title page.

Europeans witnessed with rapt attention the experiment in self-government occurring across the Atlantic. *The Federalist* was quickly recognized to be the authoritative treatise on the new American government. Thomas Jefferson, residing in Paris as Minister to France, judged it to be "the best commentary on the principles of government which was ever written."

Jean Antoine Houdon. *Benjamin Franklin,* 1778. Plaster bust. 1937.315.

On August 7 and 8, the framers debated who would be entitled to vote in national elections. Benjamin Franklin resisted the argument that only men with property should have the right to vote, because poor men would sell their votes to the rich. He reminded the Convention of the common soldiers and sailors who had fought in the War for Independence. Those captured seamen did not "redeem themselves from misery" by joining the enemy. No class had a monopoly on republican virtue. A majority of the delegates listened to Franklin's message and immediately voted against a freehold requirement in the Constitution.

V. Thirteen Contests for Ratification

47. Luther Martin. *The Genuine Information . . . Relative to the Proceedings of the General Convention Lately Held at Philadelphia.* Philadelphia, printed by Eleazer Oswald, 1788.

Luther Martin, a staunch antinationalist, had represented Maryland at the Federal Convention until August of 1787, when he returned home to gird himself for the battle against ratification. In November, he appeared before the Maryland legislature to report what had occurred at the Convention. He warned the legislators not to be fooled by the name "federal." The Convention delegates had resolved "that a national government ought to be formed," Martin revealed, and afterward they struck out "national" because they knew the word "might tend to alarm."

Afterward, Martin carried his warning to the public in a series of letters, which appeared in newspapers in at least five states. In April 1788, the letters were reprinted in a sought-after pamphlet, *The Genuine Information* . . . .

48. Letter from the Federal Republican Committee of Albany to the New York Republican Committee, April 12, 1788. Lamb Papers.

Antifederalists in Albany wrote to their allies at New York City that the publication of Luther Martin's daring letters in a pamphlet would "tend to open the Eyes of our Country more than any thing yet published."

49. Advertisement for Luther Martin's pamphlet, *The Genuine Information* . . . , in *New-York Journal and Weekly Register*, May 3, 1788. Page 3.

Advertisements for Martin's controversial pamphlet appeared frequently in newspapers from Massachusetts to South Carolina.

50. Luther Martin. Engraving, unsigned and undated.

Antifederalists hailed Martin for "daring to remove the veil of secrecy" from the Convention. Federalists insisted that his letters were filled with lies and distortions.

51. John Jay. *An Address to the People of the State of New York on the Subject of the Constitution Agreed upon at Philadelphia*. New York, printed by Samuel and John Loudon, 1788. Page 8.

In this pamphlet, Jay rebutted, point by point, the Antifederalists' assaults. On page 8, Jay insisted that "a national government competent to every national object, was indispensably necessary."

52. [Melancton Smith]. *An Address to the People of the State of New York: Showing the Necessity of Making Amendments to the Constitution . . . Previous to its Adoption*, By a Plebeian. New York, 1788. Page 23.

The "Plebeian" who signed this pamphlet was, in reality, the prominent New York City merchant Melancton Smith. In the "Postscript," Smith denied John Jay's contention that the Confederation government had failed miserably.

53. David Ramsay. *The History of the American Revolution*, 2 vols. Philadelphia, printed by R. Aitken & Son, 1789. Page 341.

David Ramsay, a South Carolina physician and historian, wrote several histories that achieved great popularity. In his *History of the American Revolution*, which appeared as the new Constitution was taking effect, Ramsay clarified what the change to a national government meant: "The fundamental distinction between the articles of confederation and the new constitution lies in this; the former acted only on the States, the latter on individuals."

54. [Mercy Otis Warren], *Observations on the New Constitution . . . , by a Columbian Patriot*, (Boston and New-York, 1788).

Late eighteenth-century mahogany arm chair with upholstered leather seat, carved splat, and square legs. Gift of Edmond B. Southwick. 1916.7.

On the afternoon of April 30, 1789, President-elect George Washington stepped onto the small balcony at Federal Hall to take the presidential oath of office. Beyond and below the railing were thousands of cheering faces. Washington bowed, then sat in this chair to wait for the crowds to quiet and the ceremony to begin.

The chair was also used by President U. S. Grant and President James Garfield at their inaugurations.

In strident, even florid language, Mercy Otis Warren admonished her fellow citizens that a strong, centralized government, lacking an adequately large legislature or a bill of rights, would reduce the people of every state to slavery. Mrs. Warren's achievements, as a poet, playwright, and historian, were exceptional for her time. Even more unusual was the recognition she received, despite her womanhood.

55. [Alexander Hamilton, John Jay, James Madison], *The Federalist: A Collection of Essays . . . ,* 2 vols. New York, printed by J. and A. M'Lean, 1788. Volume 1, pages 58–59.

James Madison's *Federalist* No. 10 is the most often quoted and discussed political treatise produced by the founders. Madison reasoned that the purpose of electing representatives was "to refine and enlarge" public opinion by passing it "through the medium of a chosen body of citizens" wise enough to "discern the true interest of their country" and patriotic enough to ignore all other considerations. A congressman's duty was not to advocate the interests and values of his own constituents but rather to govern for the good of the nation.

56. *The American Magazine, containing a Miscellaneous Collection of Original and other Valuable Essays, in Prose and Verse . . . ,* March 1788. New York, printed by S. and J. Loudon. Pages 206–207.

During the ratification controversy, this monthly magazine carried treatises, satires, and poems about the Constitution to instruct and amuse readers.

In an essay entitled "The Practice of instructing Representatives absurd and contrary to the two Principles of Liberty," a Federalist partisan, Giles Hickory, resisted Antifederalists' demands that the people ought to be able to bind their congressmen with written instructions. Such instructions would reflect the local interests and partial views of a legislator's constituents, argued Hickory, and prevent the Congress from deliberating for the public good.

57. *Observations Leading to a Fair Examination of the System of Government Proposed by the Late Convention . . . in a Number of Letters from the Federal Farmer . . .* (New York: [Thomas Greenleaf], 1787).

Mystery shrouds one of the ablest Antifederalist treatises, the letters of the Federal Farmer. Many Americans supposed that Richard Henry Lee was the Federal Farmer. Historians have cast doubts on Lee's authorship without suggesting another author. In Letter 3, the Federal Farmer protested that the House of Representatives was too small. More than sixty-five congressmen were needed to speak for every ethnic, religious, regional, and economic interest in the nation.

58. [Melancton Smith]. *An Address to the People of the State of New York: Showing the Necessity of Making Amendments to the Constitution . . . Previous to its Adoption,* By a Plebeian. New York, 1788. Page 26.

Smith urged New Yorkers to examine the new Constitution and not be awed by the reputations of the framers: "Let the Constitution stand on its own merits. If it be good, it stands not in need of great men's names to support it. If it be bad, their names ought not to sanction it."

59. *To the People of Pennsylvania,* No. 1. Signed Centinel. New York, 1788.

The most prolific Antifederalist penman signed his letters to the press "Centinel," though his real identity was probably Samuel Bryan. The letters first appeared in Philadelphia newspapers and later in a pamphlet, published in New York in 1788 and exhibited here, entitled *Observations on the Proposed Constitution for the United States of America. . . .* In Letter 1, Centinel warned that the two great men who lent their prestige to the Convention were deluded. Washington's "unsuspecting goodness" and Franklin's "weakness and attendant indecision" prevented them from seeing the Convention's sinister motives.

60. Dupré. *Benjamin Franklin,* 1784. Silver medal, made in France. Gift of James Hazen Hyde, 1947.319.

61. Richard Champion's Bristol factory. *Benjamin Franklin,* 1778. Bas relief in bisque, after a model by Caffieri. Bequest of Charles Allen Munn, 1924.94.

62. Pierre Simon Du Vivier. *George Washington*, ca. 1776. Silver medal. Gift of James Hazen Hyde, 1950.262.

The reverse side of this medal depicts the evacuation of Boston. The original gold medal was authorized by Congress, May 25, 1776.

63. *George Washington*, ca. 1777. Printed cotton kerchief, probably made in England. Bequest of Mrs. J. Insley Blair, 1952.63.

64. *Weatherwise's Federal Almanack for the Year of our Lord, 1788*. Boston, printed by John Norman.

The cover of this pocket almanack is quite rare for its picture of the Constitutional Convention. But the message conveyed was, in the opinion of Antifederalists, all too common. The framers were adored as "honour'd fathers" destined for "sublime" fame.

65. *New York Journal and Weekly Register*, November 1, 1787. Page 1.

The New York Journal and Weekly Register was one of the nation's most important Antifederalist newspapers. The editor, Thomas Greenleaf, eventually converted his newspaper from a weekly to a daily to accommodate the deluge of Antifederalist essays and satires. On November 1, readers considered the arguments of two Antifederalist spokesmen, "Cincinnatus," who may have been Richard Henry Lee, and "Brutus," who was often thought to be Robert Yates. Both deplored the omission of a bill of rights from the new Constitution. Cincinnatus called the new plan an iron trap "bated, with some illustrious names, to catch the liberties of the people."

66. [Alexander Hamilton, John Jay, James Madison], *The Federalist: A Collection of Essays . . .* , 2 vols. New York, printed by J. and A. M'Lean, 1788. Volume 2, page 349.

Hamilton insisted that in a government of enumerated and limited powers, a bill of rights was unnecessary and even "dangerous." It would "contain various exceptions to powers which are not granted; and, on this very account, would afford a colorable pretext to claim more than were granted.

For why declare that things shall not be done which there is no power to do?"

67. Jean Antoine Houdon. *Thomas Jefferson*, 1789. Plaster bust. Gift of Mrs. Laura Wolcott Gibbs, 1839.1.

Jefferson anxiously read Madison's letters describing the struggle for ratification. From France, he replied with a strong admonition that a bill of rights was what the people expected and deserved.

68. *The American Museum, or Repository of Ancient and Modern Fugitive Pieces . . .* , December 1787. Philadelphia, printed by Mathew Carey. Page 534.

The founder of this magazine, Mathew Carey, was a firm Federalist. The public demanded that he present a more balanced view of the controversy. In the issue exhibited here, he printed criticisms of the Constitution for the first time. The issue included a statement by the Virginia delegate George Mason, who refused to sign the Constitution, in part, because it lacked a bill of rights.

69. *A Review of the Constitution Proposed by the Late Convention Held at Philadelphia, 1787; By a Federal Republican*. Philadelphia, printed by Robert Smith and James Prange, 1787.

The unknown author, calling himself a "Federal Republican," alerted his countrymen that they were about to decide "the Alpha or the Omega of their political existence" and "leave a legacy of happiness or misery to their children's children." The pamphlet is unusual for its condemnation of the framers' compromise on slavery. The slave trade could be abolished in twenty years, said the author, but "what hath that to do with the abolition of slavery?" Nothing in the Constitution would prevent the nation from being "degraded" by that "impious" institution "till the end of time."

70. Ezra Ames. *Gouverneur Morris*, ca. 1815. Oil on canvas. Gift of Stephen Van Rensselaer, 1817.1. See illustration, page 55.

71. *The Constitution of the Pennsylvania Society for Promoting the Abolition of Slavery, &*

c. Philadelphia, printed by Joseph James, 1787.

On page 8 were listed the officers of the Society, including its president, Benjamin Franklin. Though he abhorred slavery and campaigned for its abolition, Franklin spoke not a word against it at the Constitutional Convention. Slavery, he conceded, was the price of union. Pennsylvania had adopted an act for the gradual abolition of slavery in 1780.

72. *The New York Journal and Weekly Register*, March 20, 1788. Page 2.

The essays of "Brutus" were among the most important Antifederalist writings. In Letter 15, the anonymous writer warned that the power of judicial review would render the courts all powerful: "The supreme court then have a right, independent of the legislature, to give a construction to the constitution . . . , and there is no power provided in this system to correct their construction or do away with it. If, therefore, the legislature pass any laws, inconsistent with the sense the judges put upon the constitution, they will declare it void; and therefore in this respect their power is superior to that of the legislature . . . The judges are supreme ———"

73. [Alexander Hamilton, John Jay, James Madison], *The Federalist: A Collection of Essays . . .* , 2 vols. New York, printed by J. and A. M'Lean, 1788. Volume 2, page 294.

In *The Federalist* No. 83, Alexander Hamilton addressed widespread fears of judicial discretion by defining the power of judicial review exclusively in terms of the written Constitution. Judicial review did not elevate the judges above the legislators but rather guaranteed that the people, whose will was expressed in the written Constitution, would remain superior to both branches.

74. *Journal of the Convention of the State of New York, Held at Poughkeepsie, in Dutchess County, the 17th of June, 1788.* Poughkeepsie, printed by Nicholas Power, 1788. Page 52.

On July 19, the Antifederalist John Lansing offered a series of clarifications and conditional amendments to the New York State ratifying convention. Among his concerns was judicial authority: "That the jurisdiction of the Supreme Court of the United States, or of any other Court to be instituted by the Congress, is not in any case to be encreased, enlarged, or extended by any fiction, collusion, or mere suggestion."

75. Christopher Gore, letter to Rufus King, October 7, 1787.

Christopher Gore, a Massachusetts lawyer who participated in the state's ratifying convention, reported to King, "The federal plan is well-esteemed and as far as can be deduced from present appearances, the adoption will be easy." Gore was overly optimistic. In February 1788, the state convention would narrowly approve the Constitution by a vote of 187 to 168.

76. Christopher Gore, letter to Rufus King, January 6, 1788.

Christopher Gore recounted a dinner conversation with the other Bostonians named as delegates to the Massachusetts ratifying convention. The Constitution "was the subject of conversation till 10 o'clock—Mr. [Samuel] Adams was open & decided agt. it." Samuel Adams argued that the system of representation in Congress was inadequate and that Congress should not have the power to lay "internal taxes," that is, taxes unrelated to trade.

77. George Washington, letter to Rufus King, February 29, 1788.

George Washington delighted in the news sent by Rufus King that Massachusetts had ratified the Constitution. Washington deemed Massachusetts an "important" state and predicted that its decision would favorably influence the undecided states. He could not predict "the fate of the Constitution" in his own state of Virginia. "I am altogether indebted to men who visit me for information respecting the disposition of the people towards it, not having gone six miles beyond the limits of my own farms since my return from Philadelphia." He mentioned the *"indefatigable* pains which some very influential characters take to oppose it."

Items 78–80 have been deleted from the exhibit.

81. *The Pennsylvania Gazette*, February 13, 1788. Page 1.

Newspaper editors responded to the public's almost insatiable desire for news and opinion about the Constitution. The entire front page of this Philadelphia newspaper was devoted to reporting the arguments being made in the Massachusetts convention for and against ratification.

82. James Madison, letter to Rufus King, June 13, 1788.

"The progress of the [Virginia] Convention is extremely slow. . . . The issue of it is more doubtful than was apprehended when I last wrote. The ostensible points of opposition are direct taxation, the imperfect representation in the House of Representatives, the equality [of states] in the Senate, regulation of trade by [a simple] majority & the Judiciary Depart[ment]."

83. James Madison, letter to Rufus King, June 22, 1788.

Madison explained to King that drafting a bill of rights, to be recommended to Congress, was a necessary strategy to conciliate some members of the opposition in Virginia. Even with this accommodation, ratification was uncertain. "How the vote will stand on the final question, I dare not positively decide. Our calculations promise us a majority of 3 or 4, possibly 5 or 6."

84. James Madison, letter to Rufus King, June 25, 1788.

"The final question in our Convention has just been decided in the affirmative by 89 ays 79 noes. Recommendatory amendments will attend the act of ratification, but are yet to be settled. The business was closed with due decorum & solemnity; and an acquiescence of the minority can not be in the least doubted."

85. Thomas Christian Lübbers. *James Madison*, after an original by Gilbert Stuart, undated [1797–1873]. Pencil on ivory. Gift of Mary Madison McGuire, 1939.243.

86. Charles Cotesworth Pinckney, letter to Rufus King, May 24, 1788.

The influential young Charles C. Pinckney attended the Constitutional Convention and, afterward, led the battle for ratification in South Carolina.

To Rufus King, he sent the happy message: "This State has ratified the federal Constitution by a majority of 149 to 73. . . . Our minority then imitated the minority in your State [Massachusetts], and declared that they would exert themselves when they returned home in reconciling the minds of their neighbors to the Constitution. . . ."

87. Asher B. Durand. *John Adams*, 1835, after Gilbert Stuart. Oil on canvas. Gift of the New York Gallery of Fine Arts, 1858.6. See illustration, page 73.

88. *The Pennsylvania Gazette*, June 13, 1787. Page 1.

John Adams's *A Defence* . . . was advertised in the Philadelphia papers as the delegates labored over a new plan of government.

One learned Philadelphian who was well acquainted with several of the delegates observed in June: "Mr. Adams' book has diffused such excellent principles among us that there is little doubt of our adopting a vigorous and compounded Federal Legislature."

89. *The Massachusetts Gazette*, April 20, 1787. Page 3.

The editor quoted from Adams's "very valuable" book one passage "well worthy the attention of every American at this important crisis of our publick affairs": "If there is one *certain truth* to be collected from the history of all ages, it is this: that the people's rights and liberties . . . can never be preserved without a strong executive, or, in other words, without separating the executive power from the legislature."

90. John Adams. *A Defence of the Constitutions of Government of the United States of America*. London, printed by C. Dilly, 1787. Rufus King's autographed copy. Volume 1, pages xvii–xviii.

The earliest state constitutions, wrote Adams, "were contrived merely by the use of reason and sense. Thirteen governments

Archibald Robertson. *Federal Hall, N.Y.C.*, 1798. Watercolor and ink on paper. Given by Sophia Minton. 1864.14.

An enthusiastic city reconstructed the war-torn building on this site in 1788–89 to welcome the new federal government. On April 30, 1789, President-elect George Washington stepped through the crimson damask that draped the central window and took the oath of office.

Congress met in Federal Hall for only a few months after the inauguration and then made the ungrateful decision to move temporarily to Philadelphia and permanently to the shores of the Potomac River. In 1804, the original home of the federal government became the first home of The New-York Historical Society.

thus founded on the natural authority of the people alone, without a pretence of miracle or mystery . . . are a great point gained in favour of the rights of mankind.''

91. John Adams. *A Defence of the Constitutions of Government of the United States of America.* London, printed by C. Dilly, 1787. Rufus King's autographed copy. Volume 2, title page.

92. John Adams. *A Defence of the Constitutions of Government of the United States of America.* London, printed by C. Dilly, 1788.

Rufus King's autographed copy. Volume 3, pages 506–7.

Adams eloquently endorsed the new United States Constitution.

93. Thomas Leman Rede. *Bibliotheca Americana; or, a chronological catalogue of the most curious and interesting books, pamphlets, state papers, & c. upon the subject of North and South America.* . . . London, printed for J. Debrett, 1789. Pages 216–17.

Among the handful of titles Rede listed as interesting and important for 1787 was the first volume of Adams's *Defence.* . . .

94. New York *Daily Advertiser*, September 21, 1787. Pages 2–3.

Philadelphia newspapers rushed to print the Constitution on September 19 and 20. New Yorkers read the new plan for the first time on September 21, when it appeared in the *Daily Advertiser* and the *New-York Packet*.

95. *The State of New York, Compiled from the Authentic Information.* New York, printed by J. Reid, 1796. A map.

In the elections for delegates to the state ratifying convention, Antifederalists captured nine of the state's thirteen counties. Federalists triumphed in New York City.

96. *To the Inhabitants of King's County.* Signed A Flatbush Farmer. New-York, printed by Francis Childs, March 23, 1788.

A Flatbush farmer recited the baneful consequences of paper money and urged his readers to elect firm Federalists to New York State's ratifying convention. The new Constitution, he reminded, provided that "no State shall emit bills of credit, make any thing but gold and silver coin a tender in payment of debts, or pass laws impairing the obligation of contracts."

97. Judge Henry Outhoudt, letter to John McKesson, April 3, 1788.

Not "since the settlement of America," wrote Judge Outhoudt, had "such exertions . . . been made upon a question of any kind as upon the new Constitution. Those who advocate the measure are engaged from morning until evening. They travel both night and day to proselyte the unbelieving antifederals———."

98. *To the Independent Electors, of the City and County of Albany.* Signed Robert M'Clallen, Chairman. Albany, printed by Charles R. Webster, March 14, 1788.

The Federalist Committee of Albany circulated this broadside, nominating candidates to the state ratifying convention, which was to meet in Poughkeepsie in June, as well as candidates for the state legislature.

99. *The Daily Advertiser*, June 4, 1788. Page 2.

New Yorkers read with interest the election results from faraway Albany and Ul-

ster counties for delegates to the state ratifying convention. In both counties, Antifederalists prevailed. The victors included Robert Yates and Governor George Clinton, who would play leading roles at the Convention.

100. Rufus King, letter to John Langdon, May 4, 1788.

When New York City elected its delegates to the state ratifying convention, Rufus King reveled in the Federalists' landslide victory. "Of three thousand votes given in this City, it is supposed that not more than two hundred were in favor of the antifederal Ticket" which was headed by Governor Clinton.

101. Painted silk banner carried in the Federal Procession at New York City, July 23, 1788. Gift of Mr. James S. Haring, 1903.12. Restored by Ms. Kathryn Scott, 1974. See illustration, page 96.

102. David Grim. *Banquet Pavilion*, undated. Watercolor on paper. Gift of Sophia Minton, 1864.17. See illustration, page 85.

103. Order of Procession in Honor of the Constitution of the United States [1788, New-York]. Broadside.

104. [Samuel Low]. *Ode for the Federal Procession upon the Adoption of the New Government.* 1788. Broadside.

"Joy to our far fam'd Chief! whose peerless worth
makes monarchs sicken at their royal birth;
And thou, grown dim with honorable age,
whose love shall grace the scientific page.
Franklin, the patriot, venerable sage. . . ."

105. *United States Constitution.* Poughkeepsie, New York, 1788. John Jay's copy, signed.

John Jay, ardent nationalist and co-author of *The Federalist*, hurried to Poughkeepsie, where the state ratifying convention assembled on June 17, 1788. On this copy of the United States Constitution, Jay noted the objections raised by the state's

Antifederalist majority and the arguments he would make in rebuttal. Jay pressed unrelentingly for unconditional ratification.

106. Alexander Robertson. *Poughkeepsie, N.Y.*, 1796. Pen-and-ink on paper. 1967.4.

107. Ezra Ames. *George Clinton*, 1814. Oil on canvas. Gift of George Clinton Tallmadge, 1858.84. See illustration, page 61.

108. John Vanderlyn. *Chancellor Robert R. Livingston*, 1804. Oil on canvas. Gift of Mrs. Thomson Livingston, 1876.1.

Robert R. Livingston, a distinguished New York City lawyer and the great-grandson of the founder of Livingston manor, ardently supported the new Constitution and defended it at the Poughkeepsie convention. This portrait was painted in Paris in 1804. Livingston was serving as Minister to France, and the artist was embarking on the most ambitious paintings of his career.

109. John McKesson. Notes of the Convention of 1788. June 17, 1788. Title page.

John McKesson was a fairly wealthy bachelor who lived in Manhattan, attended by two slaves. From 1777 to 1794 he served as clerk of the New York Assembly. In 1788, he journeyed to Poughkeepsie to become secretary of the ratifying convention. McKesson's careful notes have enabled historians to reconstruct the dramatic struggle at Poughkeepsie between Federalists and Antifederalists.

110. John McKesson. Notes of the Convention of 1788. June 18, 1788.

On June 18, the state convention agreed upon the rules of proceeding. Unlike the framers, the state delegates agreed to open the convention doors and make all their debates public.

111. John McKesson. Notes of the Convention of 1788. June 21, 1788.

On June 20, Antifederalist Melancton Smith insisted that the new House of Representatives was too small in number to represent adequately all the people of the nation. A more numerous House was required to permit men of the middling class "with the common concerns and occupations of the people" to be elected. The next day, Smith offered a formal resolution that the size of the House of Representatives be increased.

112. *The New-York Journal and Weekly Register*, July 3, 1788. Page 2.

New York City newspapers were daily filled with reports of the struggles for ratification underway in every state. On July 3, 1788, the *New York Journal* reported the Federalist victories in Virginia and New Hampshire and related the latest proceedings at Poughkeepsie.

113. John McKesson. Notes of the Convention of 1788. June 24, 1788.

Antifederalist George Livingston proposed that the state legislatures ought to be empowered to issue binding instructions to their senators and to recall any senator who disregarded the instructions. Federalist Robert R. Livingston retorted that a senator's duty was to govern for the good of the nation, not simply his own state.

114. John McKesson. Notes of the Convention of 1788. July 1, 1788.

John Jay defended empowering the new national governments to tax, rather than rely on the state governments to collect funds for the use of the central government. "National objects require national resources," Jay declared.

115. John McKesson. Notes of the Convention of 1788. July 17 [15], 1788.

On July 17, James Duane's motion to ratify the Constitution unconditionally, though with recommended amendments, was defeated 20–41. (McKesson incorrectly dated the proceedings July 15.)

116. Robert Edge Pine. *James Duane*, ca. 1784.

James Duane, a firm Federalist, was mayor of New York City from 1784 to 1789.

117. John McKesson. Notes of the Convention of 1788. July 25, 1788.

Robert Livingston concluded that the news that ten states had ratified, including important Virginia, had "changed our situation—the Confederation now closed."

118. John McKesson. Notes of the Convention of 1788. Record of voting, n.d.

On July 26, the Convention formally ratified the Constitution by a vote of 30–25. McKesson recorded the votes on each question put to the Convention. He labeled this vote 21.

119. Charles Willson Peale. *Samuel Blachley Webb*, 1779. Miniature on ivory. Gift of Colonel G. Creighton Webb, 1939.50. See illustration, page 91.

120. *The New-York Packet*, July 29, 1788. Page 2.

"Eleventh Pillar!" was the headline for this announcement that the delegates at Poughkeepsie had ratified the Constitution. Referring to the long, difficult struggle, the editor remarked that the Constitution had "undergone an ideal torture, and been preserved by fire."

121. *The Massachusetts Centinel*, August 2, 1788. See illustration, page 89.

VI. Launching
the New Government

122. Beekman family coach, ca. 1770. Gift of Gerard Beekman, 1911.25. See illustration, page 49.

123. Fragment of railing from Federal Hall. Gift of the New York Chamber of Commerce and Industry, 1884.3.

C. Milbourne. *Park Row and St. Paul's Chapel, N.Y.C.*, 1798. Watercolor on paper. 1953.63.

After the inaugural ceremonies, President George Washington stepped out of Federal Hall to be greeted by the thunderous cheers of New Yorkers. Two perfect rows of saluting militiamen formed a path to St. Paul's Chapel, where the new president walked to hear the Episcopal Bishop of New York petition the Almighty on behalf of the nation. St. Paul's stands today, the oldest church edifice in New York City. Washington's pew, kept as an historic shrine, may still be seen.

124. Late eighteenth-century arm chair used at the inauguration of President George Washington. Gift of Edmond B. Southwick, 1916.7. See illustration, page 102.

125. [Samuel Low]. *Ode to be Sung on the Arrival of the President of the United States.* 1789. Broadside.
"These shores a Head shall own,
Unsully'd by a throne,
Our much lov'd Washington,
The Great, the Good!"

126. *A Sonata, Sung by a Number of Young Girls, dressed in white and decked with wreaths and chaplets of flowers....* Trenton, April 21, 1789. (Trenton: Printed by Isaac Collins, 1789). Broadside.
On April 16, President-elect George Washington set out from Mount Vernon for New York City. At each town, honor guards and delegations of local dignitaries halted his journey. As Washington approached the bridge over Assunpink Creek, near Trenton, a triumphal arch of greenery and flowers came into view. Greeting him at the arch were the ladies and daughters of Trenton, robed in white.

127. Archibald Robertson. *Federal Hall, N.Y.C.,* 1798. Watercolor and ink on paper. Given by Sophia Minton, 1864.14. See illustration, page 107.

128. *Speech of His Excellency George Washington, Delivered to Congress upon his Introduction to Office,* May 1, 1789, New York. (Albany: Printed by C. R. & G. Webster, 1789). Broadside.

129. C. Milbourne. *Park Row and St. Paul's Chapel, N.Y.C.,* 1798. Watercolor on paper, 1953.63. See illustration, page 110.

130. Archibald Robertson. *St. Paul's Church and Brick Presbyterian Church, N.Y.C.,* 1978. Gift of Sophia Minton, 1864.15.

131. C. Milbourne. *Government House, N.Y.C.,* 1797. Watercolor on paper. X.285. See illustration, page 65.

132. Rembrandt Peale. *Mrs. George Washington,* 1853. Oil on canvas. Bequest of Caroline Phelps Stokes, 1910.2. See illustration, page 113.

Rembrandt Peale painted several portraits of Martha Washington, all closely copying a 1795 portrait executed by his father, Charles Willson Peale.

133. Gilbert Stuart. *George Washington,* after Stuart's original of 1796. Oil on canvas. Gift of Thomas J. Bryan, 1867.303.

134. Giuseppe Ceracchi. *George Clinton,* 1792. Terra-cotta bust. X.42.
Clinton had served as Governor of New York since 1778 and wielded immense patronage and political power. He campaigned tirelessly in 1788 to defeat ratification, and his opposition to the Constitution was turned against him the next year. In 1789, Robert Yates challenged him for the governorship in a bitter campaign and nearly unseated him.

135. *Fellow Citizens.* Signed A Friend to Union and the New Constitution. New York, April 30, 1789. Broadside.
George Clinton's supporters reminded the public that Yates also opposed ratifying the new plan of government. In the contest between these two Antifederalists, Clinton's men boasted that he held "the confidence of the GREAT WASHINGTON."

136. *The Federal Mechanic Ticket,* 1789. Broadside.
Advocates of Robert Yates for governor warned that the opposition candidate, incumbent George Clinton, had "manifested himself to be a *premature, decided* and *inveterate enemy*" of the Constitution.

137. *Fellow Citizens.* Signed Federalist. April 30, 1789.
"Federalist" urged the defeat of George Clinton for Governor of New York.

138. *Verses for the New Year's Day, 1789, Addressed to the Customers of the Connecticut Courant, by the Lad who Carries It.* Broadside.
A verse celebrating the launching of the new government.

139. *A Vision of the Printer's Boy.* Hartford, January 1, 1789. Broadside.
"This is the year ordain'd by fates, To rear the glory at the States."

140. *New-Year Verses of those who Carry the*

Pennsylvania Gazette to the Customers, January 1, 1790. Broadside.

This verse is unusual because its praises for the new government and its great leader, George Washington, are accompanied by harsh words for the deplorable institution of slavery.

141. *New-York Journal and Weekly Register. New-Year's Verse for 1790, . . . News-Boys's Vision.*

The poet applauded "the assembled sages" whose "noble plan" of government completed the Revolution begun by men of arms.

142–147. Two desks and four chairs used by the members of the First Congress at Federal Hall in 1789. Gift of the Corporation of the City of New York, 1837.3, .4, .7–.10.

The desks and chairs are of mahogany, fashioned in the Sheraton style.

148. Speaker's desk and lectern from the First Congress of the United States. 1958.18. See illustration, page 42.

149. *McComb Tiebout Map of New York City,* engraved by Cornelius Tiebout after a drawing by John McComb, Jr., 1789, from *The New-York Directory and Register for the Year 1789.* New York, printed for Hodge, Allen, and Campbell.

150. *The New-York Directory and Register for the Year 1789.* New York, printed for Hodge, Allen, and Campbell. Page 101.

In this eighteenth-century precursor of the telephone book, a page was set aside for the addresses of the president, vice president, and senators of the United States.

151. *An Act to Establish the Judicial Courts of the United States.* New York, printed by Thomas Greenleaf, 1789.

A printed copy of the Judiciary Act of 1789.

152. *Gazette of the United States*, September 30, 1789.

Announcing the appointment of the chief justice and associate justices of the first Supreme Court and twelve district court judges.

153. *Poor Will's Pocket Almanack for the Year 1788.* . . . Philadelphia, printed by Joseph Crukshank.

On the tiny pages of this pocket almanack, a Philadelphia man tersely recorded the daily weather conditions and little else. An exception was made on July 4, 1788: "4th-Wind at S. West, Cloudy & Very Warm. This day we had a grand procession through the City on account of the new Constitution being adopted by Ten States. . . ." The almanack's owner judged the celebration to be "such a one as never was seen in America or perhaps in any other country."

154. *The Federal Almanack,* 1789.

"On Virtue's base, by Wisdom plann'd; And rear'd by Union's sacred hand, The FEDERAL DOME, as rais'd sublime: Its PILLARS solid, strong as time; . . ."

155. C. Gore, letter to Rufus King, May 15, 1790.

A Boston man wrote to King that the appointment of John Jay as chief justice "hath delighted the people of Massachusetts. They regret that Boston was not the place of his nativity & his manners they consider so perfect as to believe that New York stole him from New England."

156. *Weatherwise's Massachusetts Almanac for the Year of our Lord, 1791.* . . . Boston, printed by Mill's & Doyle for Joseph Hovey.

A vivid cartoon and ode to the "mighty chief" George Washington appeared at the top of the page. Below were printed the schedule and meeting places of the federal circuit courts and Supreme Court.

VII. The Birth of the Bill of Rights

157. *Journal of the Convention of the State of New-York; Held at Poughkeepsie . . . June, 1788.* Poughkeepsie, printed by Nicholas Power. Pages 78–79.

Rembrandt Peale. *Mrs. George Washington* (1731–1802), 1853, after a painting by Charles Willson Peale completed in 1795. Oil on canvas. Bequest of Caroline Phelps Stokes. 1910.2.

Martha Washington's arrival in New York on May 27, 1789, occasioned a flurry of social activity and excitement. Citizens of republican tastes criticized the newspapers for calling the President's wife "Lady Washington." The Constitutional Convention and the Congress had already testified on "the insignificance of empty titles," said "A Republican."

New York Antifederalists failed in their quest to make the state's ratification conditional upon securing certain amendments to the Constitution. But the state convention did recommend amendments to Congress and instructed their own congressmen to support them. The New York proposals would have curtailed the national government's authority to tax, regulate commerce, raise armies and borrow money, barred senators from serving two consecutive terms, and permitted state legislatures to recall errant senators.

158. *The Daily Advertiser*, July 3, 1789. Page 2.

"A Pennsylvanian" supported James Madison's proposed bill of rights. Newspaper discussions of Madison's amendments were rare.

The founders' decision not to include a bill of rights in the original Constitution had aroused enormous opposition. During the ratification contest, the pages of the *Daily Advertiser* had been filled with commentary as to the need for rights amendments. But once the Constitution was ratified, Americans forgot their concern for a bill of rights and what it should include. The *Daily Advertiser* printed only four editorials on the subject between June 1789, when Madison introduced his amendments in Congress, and January 1790, when New York acted on them.

159. *The New-York Journal and Weekly Register*, August 20, 1789. Page 2.

This article, signed "A Free Mechanic" and defending Madison's proposed rights amendments, was the only commentary on the Constitution to appear in the *New-York Journal* between June 1789 and January 1790. Before ratification, the paper had been flooded with contributions about the need for a bill of rights, too many to print them all.

160. *The New-York Daily Gazette*, January 28, 1790. Page 2.

The paper reported on important debate in Congress on the meaning of freedom of the press, for which there was far less protection in 1790 than today.

Mr. Jones "hoped that something might be done, if it were possible, to discriminate between the liberty and the licentiousness of the press...." Mr. King was surprised that a gentleman so well read in the law should have any doubts upon this subject...." The freedom of the press, King said, consisted in an exemption from previous restraint. A man could print whatever he pleased, but he could also be fined and imprisoned afterwards according to the common law.

161. *The Debates and Proceedings of the Congress of the United States . . . ,* Volume 1: March 3, 1789, to February 18, 1790. Washington, D.C., printed by Gales and Seaton, 1834. Pages 779–80.

On August 17, 1789, the House of Representatives debated a provision that "no person religiously scrupulous shall be compelled to bear arms." Egbert Benson urged that any "fundamentals" be incorporated into the Constitution for the court to enforce. The fate of those who refused to bear arms was best left to the "discretion" and "humanity" of the legislature. A majority of the House disagreed with Benson and approved the provision. It was later struck out by the Senate.

162. *The Debates and Proceedings of the Congress of the United States . . . ,* Volume 1: March 3, 1789, to February 18, 1790. Washington, D.C., printed by Gales and Seaton, 1834. Pages 765–68.

One congressman proposed that the guarantees include the people's right to bind their representatives with written instructions. The majority rejected the proposal, reasoning that the purpose of a national legislature was to deliberate for the common good. The proposal was defeated 10–41.

OPPOSITE PAGE: Printed cotton kerchiefs made for the presidential election of 1888. 1944.269, X.96.

Presidential candidate Grover Cleveland and his running mate were pictured together on the Democratic kerchief. Republican Benjamin Harrison cleverly joined in the nationwide celebration of the centennial of George Washington's inauguration. Harrison passed over his running mate, Levi Morton, and chose to be pictured with the country's first president and greatest hero. Harrison won the election.

VIII. The Capital Departs
to Philadelphia

163. Francis Guy. *Tontine Coffee House, N.Y.C.,* ca. 1797 or 1803–4. Oil on canvas. 1907.32. See illustration, page 37.

164. Rufus King, memorandum addressed to [Mr.] Strong concerning the residence of Congress.

"Mr. Carroll will propose Philadelphia and Potamack for the temporary and permanent residence of Congress. It is not very probable that this arrangement will succeed. . . ." King, of course, proved to be wrong.

165. Rufus King, memorandum dated June 8, 1790, on the debates in the United States Senate regarding the location of the capital.

Anticipating a close vote, senators who advocated paying the war debts of the states rounded up their supporters to defeat an unfriendly proposal: "Mr. Johnson and Mr. Few, being notified of the question attended. Mr. Johnson came with his night cap and wrapped in many garments, attended by doctors. Bard & Romaine, and have a cot with a matras in the antechamber to repose on: by general consent the resolution was taken up—and negatived 13 to 11."

166. Rufus King, memorandum dated June 30, 1790, on the debates in the United States Senate regarding the location of the capital.

"A Bargain was made between Pennsylvania, Delaware, Maryland and Virginia to remove at the end of the Session to Philadelphia, there to remain for ten years and afterwards to remove to, and permanently remain at the Potomack."

Some New Englanders, King explained, reasoned that "the funding System, including the assumption is the primary national object; all subordinate points which oppose it must be sacrificed; the project of Philadelphia & Potomack is bad, but it will insure the funding system and the assumption."

167. "What think ye of Con__ss now [?] . . . view of the Con__ss on the road to Philadelphia." New York, 1790. Cartoon.

168. *The Carrier of Gazette of the United States,* January 1, 1790. Broadside.

Among the New Year wishes of the newsboys who carried the *Gazette* was the hope that "CONGRESS NEVER LEAVE THE CITY."

IX. The Founders:
Heroes or Partisans?

169. *The mourning of George Washington.* Printed cotton kerchief by John Macke & Cory Glascow, ca. 1800. Gift of Mrs. J. Insley Blair, 1941.106.

170. *The death of General Washington.* Printed cotton kerchief by Pemker & Lazard, Scotland, ca. 1800. Gift of Mrs. J. Insley Blair, 1942.536.

171. *Britannia presenting an olive branch to General Washington.* Printed cotton kerchief by B. Warren, London, ca. 1800. Bequest of Mrs. J. Insley, 1952.59.

172. *The mourning of Alexander Hamilton.* Printed linen, made in the United States, ca. 1805–6. 1967.51.

173. Ralph Wood, Jr. *Benjamin Franklin,* ca. 1790. Staffordshire glazed statuette. Bequest of Charles Allen Munn, 1924.89.

174. Devaulx. *George Washington,* late 18th century. Bronze statuette, made in France. Bequest of Charles Allen Munn, 1924.71.

175. Ralph Wood, Jr. *Benjamin Franklin,* ca. 1800. Staffordshire glazed pottery statuette. Bequest of Charles Allen Munn, 1924.60.

Photograph of the Naval Parade at New York City, April 29, 1889.

On April 29, 1889, New Yorkers embarked on a grand, three-day commemoration of the inauguration of President George Washington and the launching of the new federal government in 1789. The festivities began at 11:00 A.M. with a naval parade from Elizabethport, down the East River, around the Battery, and onward to Governor's Island. President Harrison, Cabinet officials, and other dignitaries sailed on the steamer *U.S.S. Dispatch*, surrounded by a throng of naval vessels, yachts, steamboats, and tugs. At the conclusion of the parade, a crew of shipmasters from the Marine Society of the Port of New York, with Captain Ambrose Snow as coxswain, rowed the President ashore. Members of the same society had rowed President Washington from Elizabethport to the foot of Wall Street one hundred years earlier.

The European maker labeled this figure "Washington" in error.

176. *Let Every True Whig Read this with Attention. To the Electors of the City and County of New York.* [New York, 1791].

This broadside in support of Thomas Jefferson vilified his opponents as "sons of Mammon."

X. The Centennial Celebration, 1889

177–193. Seventeen photographs and artifacts from the 1889 centennial celebration of George Washington's inauguration. See illustrations above and on page 115.

XI. Making the People Sovereign

194. Thomas Jefferson. *Notes on the State of Virginia*. London, printed for John Stockdale, 1787. Pages 125, 128.

Jefferson recalled that the Virginia Constitution of 1776 "was formed when we were new and inexperienced in the science of good government." The ordinary state legislature framed the constitution, declared it to be in effect, and then went on with its other legislative business. In 1776 few people understood, as Jefferson did, that a constitution written and approved by the legislature could not be expected to limit legislative power in any practical sense.

195. *A constitution or frame of government, agreed upon by the Delegates of the People of the state of Massachusetts-Bay. . . .* Boston, printed by Benjamin Edes & Sons, 1780.

It was in this 1780 constitution that the phrase "We the people" was used for the first time. The framers of the United States Constitution built on the achievements in Massachusetts when they devised the special ratifying and amending procedures to make the United States Constitution a fundamental law.

196. James Wilson. *Introductory Lecture to a Course of Law Lectures. . . .* Philadelphia, printed by T. Dobson, 1791. Pages 32–33.

Wilson, a framer, Supreme Court justice, and distinguished professor of law, explained how the special ratifying and amending procedures devised by the Convention made the theory of popular sovereignty a legal reality.

197. *The Constitution of the Commonwealth of Pennsylvania*. Philadelphia, printed by Z. Poulson, Jr., 1790.

In 1790, Pennsylvania adopted a new frame of government created in the image of the United States Constitution. This copy belonged to Albert Gallatin, one of the framers of the Pennsylvania constitution.

Notes

1. James Thomas Flexner, *George Washington and the New Nation (1783-1793)* (Boston: Little, Brown & Co., 1970), 110; J. M. to Thomas Jefferson, July 27, 1787, in Julian P. Boyd, ed., *Papers of Thomas Jefferson* (Princeton: Princeton University Press, 1950–), 11: 631.

2. Flexner, *George Washington*, 107; David Humphreys to G. W., January 20, 1787, quoted in Charles Warren, *The Making of the Constitution* (New York: Barnes & Noble, 1967), 64.

3. J. M. to G. W., December 7, 1786, in William T. Hutchinson, ed., *Papers of James Madison* (Chicago: University of Chicago Press, 1962–85), 9:199; J. M. to Edmund Randolph, April 15, 1787, ibid., 378; Henry Knox to Marquis de Lafayette, quoted in Flexner, *George Washington*, 111.

4. G. W. to J. M., November 5, 1786, *Papers of James Madison*, 9:161; J. M. to William Gordon, July 8, 1783, quoted in Warren, *Making of the Constitution*, 12; G. W. to John Jay, August 1, 1786, quoted in Warren, *Making of the Constitution*, 18.

5. G. W., Message to the State Governors, June 8, 1763, quoted in Warren, *Making of the Constitution*, 13; G. W. to J. M., March 31, 1787, *Papers of James Madison*, 9:342–44.

6. Flexner, *George Washington*, 110: John J. Fitzpatrick, ed., *The Diaries of George Washington* (Boston: Houghton Mifflin Co., 1925), 3:214–16.

7. Irving Brant, *James Madison, Father of the Constitution, 1787-1800* (New York: Bobbs-Merrill Co., 1950), 20 n. 19.

8. Clinton Rossiter, *1787: The Grand Convention* (New York: Macmillan Co., 1965), 125.

9. J. M. to G. W., April 16, 1787, *Papers of James Madison*, 9:382–84; J. M. to Thomas Jefferson, March 19, 1786, *Papers of James Madison*, 9:317–22; J. M. to Edmund Randolph, April 8, 1787, *Papers of James Madison*, 9:368–71; J. M., "Vices of the Political System of the U. States," *Papers of James Madison*, 9:348–52.

10. *Papers of James Madison*, 9:352–57.

11. J. M. to Thomas Jefferson, March 19, 1786, *Papers of James Madison*, 9:318.

12. Ibid., 9:356–57.

13. Warren, *Making of the Constitution*, 23–29, 45, 65.

14. *Papers of James Madison*, 9:356–57.

15. Ibid., 357.

16. J. M. to George Muter, January 7, 1787, *Papers of James Madison*, 9:231; Warren, *Making of the Constitution*, 72–73; Thomas Jefferson to J. M., January 30, 1787, *Papers of James Madison*, 9:247–48.

17. J. M. to Thomas Jefferson, May 15, 1787, *Papers of James Madison*, 9:415.

18. Edmund Randolph to J. M., March 27, 1787, *Papers of James Madison*, 9:415; Edmund Randolph to the Speaker, Virginia House of Delegates, October 10, 1787, in Jonathan Elliot, ed., *The Debates in the Several State Conventions on the Adoption of the Federal Constitution*, 2nd ed., rev. (Philadelphia: J. B. Lippincott Co., 1888), 1:482; J. M. to G. W., April 16, 1787, *Papers of James Madison*, 9:383.

19. J. M. to James Madison, Sr., May 27, 1787, *Papers of James Madison*, 10:10; G. W. to Arthur Lee, May 20, 1787, *The Records of the Federal Convention of 1787*, rev. ed. (New Haven: Yale University Press, 1974), 3: 22; Rufus King to Jeremiah Wadsworth, May 24, 1787, *Records*, 3:26.

20. *Records*, 1:2.

21. J. M. to S. H. Smith, February 2, 1827, *Records*, 1:475; Ed. note, *Records*, 1:7–9; Warren, *Making of the Constitution*, 800–2.

22. *Records*, 1:7; Catherine Drinker Bowen, *Miracle at Philadelphia* (Boston: Little, Brown & Co., 1966), 34.

23. *Records*, 1:7–13.

24. *Records*, 1:10, 15, 17; Warren, *Making of the Constitution*, 303; Thomas Jefferson to John Adams, August 30, 1787, *Records*, 3:76; *Pennsylvania Packet and Daily Advertiser*, August 22, 1787; J. M. to Thomas Jefferson, July 18, 1786, *Papers of James Madison*, 10: 105.

25. *Records*, 1:9, 17; Gentlemen of Rhode Island to the Chairman of the Convention, May 11, 1787, *Records*, 3:18–19.

26. George Mason to Arthur Lee, May 21, 1787, *Records*, 3:24; on the Maryland delegates, see Rossiter, *Grand Convention*, 112–16.

27. J. M. to William Short, June 6, 1787, *Records*, 3:36–37; J. M. to Thomas Jefferson, June 6, 1787, *Records*, 3:35–36; Thomas Jefferson to John Adams, August 30, 1787, *Records*, 3:76; Benjamin Rush to Richard Price, June 12, 1787, *Records*, 3:33.

28. Benjamin Franklin to Thomas Jefferson, April 19, 1787, *Papers of Thomas Jefferson*, 2:302; G. W. to John Jay, August 1, 1786, quoted in Warren, *Making of the Constitution*, 17; George Mason to George Mason, Sr., June 1, 1787, *Records*, 3:32–3.

29. *Records*, 1:134.

30. [Alexander Hamilton, John Jay, James Madison], in Clinton Rossiter, ed., *The Federalist Papers*, (New York: New American Library, 1961), No. 31 [Hamilton], 193; James Wilson, *The Works of the Honorable James Wilson*, Bird Wilson, ed. (Philadelphia: Bronson and Chauncey, 1804), 1:6, 9–10; James Wilson, L. L. D. and Thomas McKean, L. L. D., *Commentaries on the Constitution* . . . (London: J. Debrett et al., 1792), 29; *Federalist*, No. 1 [Hamilton], 33.

31. John Adams, *A Defence of the Constitutions of Government of the United States of America* (London: C. Dilly, 1787–88), 3:504–5.

32. *Records*, 1:18.

33. Elizabeth P. McCaughey, *From Loyalist to Founding Father: The Political Odyssey of William Samuel Johnson* (New York: Columbia University Press, 1980), 212.

34. *Records*, 1:20–22.

35. Ibid., 530.

36. Ibid., 33–35.

37. Ibid., 35–38; Rossiter, *Grand Convention*, 111.

38. *Records*, 1:53–54.

39. James Wilson, *Considerations on the Nature and Extent of the Legislative Authority of the British Parliament* (Philadelphia: Bradford's, 1774); *Records*, 1:69.

40. J. M. to Edmund Randolph, April 8, 1787, *Papers of James Madison*, 9:370; Notes for a Speech . . . , June [14 or 21], 1784, *Papers of James Madison*, 9:385; Resolutions proposed by Mr. Randolph in Convention, *Records*, 1:20–23; [J. M.], *Records*, 1:138.

41. *Records*, 1:65.

42. Ibid., 69; ibid., 2:35; ibid., 1:80; *Federalist*, No. 68 [Hamilton], 412–14; *Federalist*, No. 71 [Hamilton], 432.

43. *Records*, 1:80–81.

44. Ibid., 65–66, 74, 113.

45. Ibid., 65, 254.

46. James Wilson, *Works*, R. G. McCluskey, ed. (Cambridge: Harvard University Press, 1967), 1:318–19; *Records*, 1:97.

47. *Records*, 1:96.

48. Thomas Paine, *Common Sense* (Philadelphia: 1776).

49. *Pennsylvania Gazette*, August 15, 1787, in *Commentaries on the Constitution*, 1:187.

50. Pierce Butler to Weedon Butler, May 5, 1788, *Records*, 3:302; *Records*, 1:103.

51. Gouverneur Morris to G. W., October 30, 1787, quoted in Warren, *Making of the Constitution*, 730.

52. Sherman, *Records*, 1:65, 85; Mason, *Records*, 1: 86; *Records*, 1:88.

53. Mason, *Records*, 2:65.

54. J. M., *Records*, 2:550.

55. Wilson, *Records*, 1:98; Sherman, *Records*, 1:99; Mason, *Records*, 1:101–2.

56. P. Butler to Weedon Butler, May 5, 1788, *Records*, 3:301–2.

57. J. M., *Records*, 1:138–39, 2:74; Wilson, *Records*, 2:73; Mason, *Records*, 2:78.

58. Charles Grove Haines, *The American Doctrine of Judicial Supremacy* (New York: Russell & Russell, 1959); Julius Goebel, Jr., *History of the Supreme Court*, vol. 1, *Antecedents and Beginnings to 1801* (New York: Macmillan Co., 1971), 103–4.

59. Gerry, *Records*, 1:97–98; 2:74–75; Nathaniel Gorham and Luther Martin, 2:73, 76; *Federalist*, No. 73 [Hamilton], 446–47.

60. Gordon Wood, *The Creation of the American Republic, 1776-1787* (New York: W. W. Norton, 1969), 242–43, 274–79, 306–308, 340; Virginia Constitution of 1776, in Francis N. Thorpe, ed., *The Federal and State Constitutions* . . . (Washington, D.C.: U.S. Government Printing Office, 1909), 7:3815ff.; Thomas Jefferson, Query 13, *Notes on the State of Virginia* (Philadelphia: Prichard & Hall, 1788); for the Massachusetts documents, see Jack P. Greene, *Colonies to Nation, 1763-1789* (New York: W. W. Norton, 1967), 347–57.

61. *Records*, 2:88, 92–93.

62. *Records*, 1:123; 2:89, 90.

63. *Records*, 1:123, 335; 2:91, 476.

64. *Federalist*, No. 22 [Hamilton], 152; *Federalist*, No. 53 [J. M.], 331.

65. *Federalist*, No. 78 [Hamilton], 467–68.

66. *Records*, 3:552; 1:45–46, 132, 339.

67. *Records*, 1:48–50, 132–33.

68. *Records*, 1:48–50, 132–34.

69. Ibid., 49–50; *Federalist*, No. 10 [J. M.], 77–84; *Federalist*, No. 57 [J. M.], 354.

70. *Records*, 1:137.

71. *Federalist*, No. 57, 350.

72. *Records*, 1:50, 51, 151.

73. Ibid., 52, 150, 153.

74. Ibid., 52, 53.

75. Ibid., 151, 154, 136.

76. Ibid., 136, 156.

77. Ibid., 179, 169.

78. Ibid., 179, 200–201.

79. Roger Sherman made the proposal before the voting rule in the lower house had been decided. Ibid., 196, 202.

80. Ibid., 87.

81. Ibid., 235–37.

82. Ibid., 240.

83. Luther Martin, *The Genuine Information . . .* (1788), *Records*, 3:178–79.

84. Paterson, *Records*, 1:178, 250.

85. Ibid., 242.

86. Ibid., 242–45.

87. Ibid., 254.

88. Ibid., 318–19.

89. Ibid., 252, 317, 256.

90. Ibid., 288–93.

91. Ibid.

92. Warren, *Making of the Constitution*, 228, 229.

93. Richard B. Morris, ed., *Alexander Hamilton and the Founding of the Nation* (New York: Dial Press, 1957), 159; Gerald Stourzh argues that the speech was the greatest of Hamilton's career, setting forth his lifelong political principles (see his *Alexander Hamilton and the Idea of Republican Government* [Stanford: Stanford University Press, 1970], 39). See also *Records*, 1:293 n. 9.

94. James Thomas Flexner, *The Young Hamilton: A Biography* (Boston: Little, Brown & Co., 1978), 335; Rossiter, *Grand Convention*, 178.

95. *Records*, 1:322.

96. Ibid., 255.

97. Ibid., 343, 355.

98. Wood, *Creation*, 165–67.

99. *Records*, 1:214–15.

100. Ibid., 360–62.

101. Ibid., 218–19, 289, 398–409, 411.

102. Ibid., 409, 423.

103. Ibid., 425, 426.

104. Ibid., I:463–64, 466.

105. Ibid., 468–69.

106. Ibid., 482, 491–93.

107. Ibid., 510. Warren provides a complete discussion of how several delegates later recollected the event (see *Making of the Constitution*, 262 n. 2).

108. *Records*, 1:511, 515.

109. Ibid., 516, 566.

110. G. W. to Alexander Hamilton, July 10, 1787, in John C. Fitzpatrick, ed., *The Writings of George Washington* (Washington, D.C.: U.S. Government Printing Office, 1931–44), 29:245; *Records*, 1:486, 588, 593, 595, 597.

111. Ibid., 597; 2:350; speech of Rufus King to the United States Senate in Charles R. King, ed., *The Life and Correspondence of Rufus King* (New York: G. P. Putnam's Sons, 1894–1900), 6:697–700; *Pollock v. Farmers Loan and Trust Co.* (1895), 158 U. S. 601.

112. *Records*, 1:560, 578, 583; 2:3.

113. Luther Martin, *The Genuine Information; Records*, 2:15, 19–20; William Samuel Johnson to Samuel Peters, *Records*, 4:72–73; Rossiter, *Grand Convention*, 197.

114. *Records*, 2:17, 27.

115. Ibid., 27–29; J. M. to Thomas Jefferson, October 24, 1787, *Papers of James Madison*, 10:212.

116. *Records*, 2:376, 440.

117. J. M. to Thomas Jefferson, October 24, 1787, *Papers of James Madison*, 10:212.

118. *Records*, 1:164–68.

119. Ibid., 2:29.

120. Ibid., 2:29, 32; Richard Hofstadter, *The Idea of a Party System: The Rise of Legitimate Opposition in the United States, 1780-1840* (Berkeley: University of California Press, 1969). James Caesar reminds us of the lesson first articulated by Martin Van Buren, that a system of legitimate national party competition ensured that there would be candidates with continental reputations and that the House would, therefore, rarely be called on to select the president. The collapse of the first party system yielded an array of aspirants for the presidents' office in 1824 and no party discipline to renew the field to two respectable candidates. James W. Caesar, *Presidential Selection* (Princeton: Princeton University Press, 1969), 252.

121. *Records*, 2:30–31.

122. Ibid., 32.

123. Ibid., 100, 120.

124. Wilson, *Records*, 2:102; Gouverneur Morris, *Records*, 2:103–4; Sherman, *Records*, 1:68; Gouverneur Morris, *Records*, 2:29, 31; Pinckney, "Observations on the Plan of Government . . ." (1787), *Records*, 3:110–11; Morris, *Records*, 2:53–54; J. M. to Thomas Jefferson, October 24, 1787, *Papers of James Madison*, 10:208–9; *Federalist*, No. 72 [Hamilton], 437–38.

125. *Records*, 2:54–56.

126. Ibid., 57–58; Gerry, *Records*, 2:114.

127. *Records*, 2:32, 63, 64.

128. *Records*, 2:102–3, 115, 120.

129. *Federalist*, No. 68, 412–14.

130. Ibid.; Hugh Williamson, *Records*, 2:59; Caesar, *Presidential Selection*, 50, 65, 236–37, 242, 247, 250.

131. *Records*, 2:95.

132. James Madison, Sr., to J. M., August 1, 1787, *Papers of James Madison*, 10:120–21; Warren, *Making of the Constitution*, 368.

133. Diary of G. W., July 30, 31, 1787, in Fitzpatrick, *Diaries of George Washington*, 3:230.

134. *Records*, 2:163–75, 176.

135. Ibid., 137.

136. *Records*, 1:53.

137. Ibid., 2:163–75; Richard Henry Lee to J. M., August 11, October 10, 1785, in James Curtis Ballagh, ed., *The Letters of Richard Henry Lee* (New York: Macmillan Co., 1914), 2:383, 389.

138. *Records*, 2:221–24.

139. Ibid., 163–64.

140. Chilton Williamson, *American Suffrage: From Property to Democracy 1760-1860* (Princeton: Princeton University Press, 1960), 76–116; Warren, *Making of the Constitution*, 400; Wood, *Creation*, 168–69.

141. *Records*, 2:201–6.

142. Ibid., 216.

143. Wood, *Creation*, 208–22; Warren, *Making of the Constitution*, 416–17.

144. *Records*, 2:121–22, 123.

145. Ibid., 248–49.

146. Ibid., 249–51; Timothy Pickering to Charles Tillinghast, December 24, 1787, quoted in Warren, *Making of the Constitution*, 419.

147. *Records*, 2:318–19, 344–45, 348–50.

148. Ibid., 359–63.

149. Ibid., 364.

150. Bernard Bailyn, *The Ideological Origins of the American Revolution* (Cambridge: Harvard University Press, 1967), 232–46.

151. *Records*, 2:364, 369–71.

152. Ibid., 373–75.

153. Ibid., 400, 446.

154. James Wilson to Pennsylvania Convention, December 3, 1787, *Records*, 3:161.

155. Patrick Henry, *Debates*, 3:455–56.

156. *Records*, 2:428–29; *Federalist*, No. 22, 151.

157. *Records*, 2:428, 430.

158. Ibid., 299, 423, 430, 547; Gouvernour Morris to Timothy Pickering, December 22, 1814, *Records*, 3:420.

159. *Records*, 1:100–101; *Records*, 2:298–99; Charles Warren, *Congress, Constitution, and the Court* (Boston: Little, Brown & Co., 1925), 50–51, n. 1.

160. Goebel, *Antecedents*, 137–41; Haines, *American Doctrine*, 105–12.

161. Julius Goebel, Jr., ed., *The Law Practice of Alexander Hamilton* (New York: Columbia University Press, 1964), 1:282–543; Goebel, *Antecedents*, 132–39; Wood, *Creation*, 457–59; Haines, *American Doctrine*, 99–104.

162. James Monroe to J. M., November 22, 1788, *Papers of James Madison*, 11:361.

163. [Richard Henry Lee], "Letters from a Federal Farmer," in Herbert J. Storing, ed., *The Complete Antifederalist* (Chicago: University of Chicago Press, 1981), 2:315–16, 322; "Essays of 'Brutus,' " *New York Journal* (October 1787–April 1, 1788), in *Complete Antifederalist*, 2:419, 422.

164. *Federalist*, No. 81 [Hamilton], 482; ibid., No. 78, 466–71.

165. *Records*, 2:27–29.

166. Patrick Henry, *Debates*, 3:156; *Records*, 2:439–43.

167. Ibid.

168. Warren, *Making of the Constitution*, 425.

169. *Records*, 2:476–77.

170. Ibid., 478–79, 560.

171. *Federalist*, No. 42 [J. M.], 252–53.

172. *Records*, 2:318.

173. "To the Freeman of the United States," signed Harrington, in *Massachusetts Centinel*, June 9, 1787, and *Connecticut Courant*, June 11, 1787; *Connecticut Courant*, August 20, 1787.

174. *Records*, 2:496–500.

175. Ibid., 500, 511–13.

176. Ibid., 522, 525.

177. Ibid., 389, 539.

178. J. M. to Thomas Jefferson, October 24, 1787, *Records*, 3:131–33; *Federalist*, No. 48 [J. M.], 309–310.

179. *Federalist*, No. 71 [Hamilton], 433; *Federalist*, No. 70 [Hamilton], 424.

180. Ibid., No. 68 [Hamilton], 411; "An Old Soldier," *Connecticut Gazette*, January 4, 1788, in John Kaminski and Gaspare J. Saladino, eds., *Commentaries on the Constitution, Public and Private* (Madison, Wisc.: State Historical Society, 1984), 3:256–57; "Letters of Cato," 4, in *Complete Antifederalist*, 2:114; Luther Martin, *Debates*, 3:484–85; *Federalist*, No. 71, 432–34; Phillip Bradley, ed., *Alexis de Tocqueville: Democracy in America* (New York: A. A. Knopf, 1945), 1:137–39.

181. *Tocqueville: Democracy in America*, 1:136–38.

182. *Records*, 1:122, 202–3; *Records*, 1:559, 629–30.

183. Adams, *Defence of the Constitutions*, 3:506–7.

184. *Tocqueville: Democracy in America*, 1:104.

185. Bruce Ackerman, "Discovering the Constitution," The Storrs Lectures, *Yale Law Journal*, 93:6 (May 1984).

186. John Hart Ely, *Democracy and Distrust: A Theory of Judicial Review* (Cambridge: Harvard University Press, 1981), 49, 65, 218–19 n. 12.

187. *Records*, 2:547.

188. Ibid., 565–80; Ezra Stiles, "The Literary Diary of Ezra Stiles," *Records*, 3:293–95; Gouverneur Morris to Moss Kent, January 12, 1815, *Records*, 3:420–21; J. M. to Jared Sparks, April 18, 1831, *Records*, 3:499.

189. *Records*, 2:196, 477.

190. Ibid., 590.

191. Ibid., 585–87.

192. Ibid., 614–15.

193. Ibid., 588.

194. Ibid., 617–18.

195. James Otis, *The Rights of the British Colonies Asserted and Proved* (Boston: Edes and Gill, 1764); Massachusetts Circular Letter, February 11, 1768, in Greene, *Colonies to Nation*, 347–48; Resolution of the Stamp Act Congress, *Colonies to Nation*, 63–64; Declaration of Rights and Grievances, October 14, 1774, in Worthington C. Ford, ed., *Journals of the Continental Congress* (Washington, D.C.: U.S. Government Print-

ing Office, 1904–36), 1:63–74. Not all American patriots, however, believed that the law actually provided a remedy for Parliamentary oppression. See Richard Bland, *An Inquiry into the Rights of the British Colonies . . .* (Williamsburg: Alexander Purdie and Co., 1766). Legal scholars in search of an American tradition of unwritten constitutional law have seized upon the prominence of the national law idiom in the legal arguments of the revolutionaries to demonstrate the historical roots and legitimacy of today's expansive, extraconstitutional judicial decision making. Such arguments overlook the dramatic change that occurred after independence. See Thomas Grey, "Origins of the Unwritten Constitution: Fundamental Law in American Revolutionary Thought," *Stanford Law Review*, 30: 843–49; Edward Corwin, *Corwin on the Constitution*, ed. Richard Loss (Ithaca: Cornell University Press, 1981), 200.

196. Thomas Jefferson to J. M., March 5, 1789, *Papers of Thomas Jefferson*, 14:659–61; J. M. to Thomas Jefferson, October 17, 1788, ibid., 18–20.

197. *Federalist*, No. 84 [Hamilton], 513.

198. Henry, *Debates*, 3:44, 49; Monroe, *Debates*, 3: 218; Mason, *Debates*, 3:271; Randolph, *Debates*, 3:468.

199. Mason, Nicholas, and Randolph; *Debates*, 3: 444–45, 468; Theophilus Parson, *Debates*, 2:443, reprinted in Wood, *Creation of the American Republic*, 538; "Letters from a Federal Farmer," VIII, 196, reprinted in *Complete Antifederalist*, 2:324; Jefferson, *Notes on Virginia*, Query 17; Jefferson to J. M., December 20, 1787, *Papers of Thomas Jefferson*, 12:439–40; Wilson, *Debates*, 2:436, 453.

200. J. M. to Thomas Jefferson, October 17, 1788, *Papers of Thomas Jefferson*, 14:18–19; J. M., June 8, 1789, *Annals of the Congress of the United States . . . March 3, 1789 to May 27, 1824* (Washington, D.C.: Gales and Seaton, 1834–56), 2:258, 439.

201. J. M. to Thomas Jefferson, December 8, 1788, ibid., 340.

202. J. M., June 8, August 15, 1789, *Annals*, 1:432, 436–47, 439, 730; "Notes for a Speech in Congress," ca. June 8, 1789, *Papers of James Madison*, 12:193–95.

203. *Records*, 2:629–30.

204. Ibid., 630–31.

205. Ibid., 631–33; see also 479–563, 644–45, 646–47.

206. Ibid., 641–43.

207. Ibid., 643–44.

208. Ibid., 644–47.

209. Ibid., 648.

210. *Maryland Journal*, March 7, 1788; J. M. to Thomas Jefferson, July 19, 1787, *Records*, 3:60; *New York Daily Advertiser*, August 14, 1787; Warren, *Making of the Constitution*, 138–39, 183, 337–38, 354–55.

211. *Pennsylvania Evening Herald*, June 8, 1787, *New Haven Gazette*, August 2, 1787; *Massachusetts Centinel*, August 8, 1787; a Philadelphia newspaper quoted in Warren, *Making of the Constitution*, 183.

212. J. M. to Thomas Jefferson, October 24, 1787, *Records*, 3:131–36; *Federalist*, No. 37 [J. M.], 230.

213. Ibid., No. 1 [Hamilton], 33.

214. George Washington to Bushrod Washington, November 10, 1787, *Writings of George Washington*, 29: 311–12.

215. Donald Jackson, ed., *Diaries of George Washington* (Charlottesville, Va.: University of Virginia Press, 1976–80), 5:185.

216. Stephen Mix Mitchell to William Samuel Johnson, July 20, 1787, William Samuel Johnson Papers, Connecticut Historical Society; Philip Jordan, Jr., "Connecticut's Politics During the Revolution and Confederation, 1776–1789," Ph.D. diss., Yale University, 1962.

217. Wood, *Creation*, pts. 1 and 2.

218. *Records*, 1:34–35, 86–87, 178, 410–13.

219. Hannah Fenichel Pitkin, *The Concept of Representation* (Berkeley: University of California Press, 1967), 216–17.

220. Pitkin, *The Concept of Representation*, citing Lewis Anthony Dexter, "The Representative and his District," *Human Organization*, XVI (Spring 1957).

221. Tocqueville, *Democracy in America*, 1:207–8, 210; Edmund Burke, "A Representative's Duty to Constituents" in *The New York Times*, October 18, 1984, A27.

222. *Records*, 1:51, 318–19; *Federalist*, No. 37, 227; *Federalist*, No. 44 [J. M.], 282; *Federalist*, No. 85 [Hamilton], 521–22; [J. M.], *Papers of James Madison*, 9:355–56.

223. *Federalist*, No. 10, 79, 80; Pitkin, *Concept of Representation*, 191–97.

224. *Records*, 1:53; *Federalist*, No. 10, 81, 82. Among modern criticisms of *Federalist* No. 10, one of the most widely read is Robert Dahl's *A Preface to Democratic Theory* (Chicago: University of Chicago Press, 1956), but Dahl does not realize how much he and Madison think alike.

225. For an interesting discussion of America's new self-assessment after the war, see Wood, *Creation*, 606–15.

226. *Federalist*, No. 10, 82.

227. *Records*, 1:20.

228. Ibid., 48, 132, 359.

229. Ibid., 48–50, 132–33; J. M. to Thomas Jefferson, October 24, 1787, *Papers of Thomas Jefferson*, 12: 27.

230. *Records*, 2:217.

231. *Federalist*, No. 10, 82–83.

232. Melancton Smith, *Debates*, 2:245–48, 259–60; John Lansing, Jr., *Debates*, 2:217, 220; John Smith, *Debates*, 2:229; John Williams, *Debates*, 2:242; Mason, *Debates*, 3:30–32, 262; Henry, *Debates*, 3:164–65, 396; John Taylor, *Debates*, 2:36; Francis Dana, *Debates*, 2: 37–38.

233. Wilson, *Debates*, 2:473–74; *Federalist*, No. 35 [Hamilton], 214–15.

234. J. G. A. Pocock, "The Classical Theory of Deference," *American Historical Review*, 81 (June 1976), 516–23.

235. Wood, *Creation*, 562.

236. *Federalist*, No. 35, 214–15; *Federalist*, No. 55 [J. M.], 341.

237. *Federalist*, No. 10, 79, 82.

238. Ibid., No. 57, 350; No. 55, 341.

239. Noah Webster, quoted in Storing, *Complete Antifederalist*, 1:45; Hamilton, *Debates*, 2:265; Wilson, *Debates*, 2:58.

240. *Records*, 1:214–15; Wood, *Creation*, 166.

241. Fisher Ames, *Debates*, 2:7–12.

242. *Annals*, 1:733–47.

243. *Federalist*, No. 46 [J. M.], 296–97.

244. *Records*, 1:48, 421.

245. Ibid.; see also Gouverneur Morris, *Records*, 2:52.

246. *Federalist*, No. 62 [J. M.], 379.

247. *Records*, 1:51, 151–52, 421–23.

248. Ibid., 214–15, 421–26; *Federalist*, No. 62, 378–79.

249. *Federalist*, No. 62, 379.

250. [Robert Yates—attribution disputed], "Essays of 'Brutus,' " 2:444; *Debates*, 2:45–48, 137, 160.

251. *Federalist*, No. 39 [J. M.], 244; see also *Federalist*, No. 9 [Hamilton], 76.

252. *Records*, 1:51–52, 406–8.

253. Ibid., 2:8–9; ibid., 1:37, 48, 50, 155.

254. *Federalist*, No. 62, 337.

255. *Records*, 2:4–5, 94.

256. Ibid., 1:427–28.

257. Ibid., 2:290–92.

258. *Debates*, 2:289.

259. Ibid., 289, 293, 311.

260. Ibid., 296.

261. Ibid., 433–34; *Records*, 1:153–54; see also Charles Pinckney, *Records*, 1:397–404; *Federalist*, No. 14: 101; 63:389 [J. M.]; Wood, *Creation*, 560–61.

262. *Records*, 1:288–90, 511–14.

263. Ibid., 233–34; see 419.

264. Ibid., 527, 529, 543–47; *Federalist*, No. 37, 229.

265. *Records*, 2:224–25, 233–34.

266. Storing, "What the Anti-Federalists Were For," *Complete Antifederalist*, 58–59; [Lee?], "Letters from the Federal Farmer," in Storing, *Complete Antifederalist*, 2:287.

267. Storing, *Complete Antifederalist*, 58.

268. *Debates*, 3:164; see also Henry, *Debates*, 3:59, 326, 385; Samuel Thompson, *Debates*, 2:32; William Symmes, *Debates*, 2:72.

269. Henry, *Debates*, 3:164, 326; Randolph, *Debates*, 3:70, 123.

270. *Federalist*, No. 10, 78–80; *Federalist*, No. 51 [J. M.], 322.

271. *Debates*, 3:225.

272. Wood, *Creation*, 53–54, 183.

273. *Federalist*, No. 14, 103–4; see also John Marshall, *Debates*, 3:232.